Kingdom Come

John V. Taylor

KINGDOM COME

SCM PRESS
London
TRINITY PRESS INTERNATIONAL
Philadelphia

First published 1989

SCM Press
26–30 Tottenham Road
London N1 4BZ

Trinity Press International
3725 Chestnut Street
Philadelphia, Pa. 19104

British Library Cataloguing in Publication Data

Taylor, John V. (John Vernon, 1914–)
 Kingdom come.
 1. Bible. Special subjects: Christian doctrine. Kingdom of
 God
 I. Title
 231.7'2

ISBN 0–334–00841–7

Library of Congress Cataloging-in-Publication Data

Taylor, John Vernon, 1914–
 Kingdom come / John V. Taylor.
  p. cm.
 ISBN 0 334 00841 7
 1. Kingdom of God. I. Title.
BT94.T39   1989
231.7'2—dc20   89–35974

Typeset at The Spartan Press Ltd, Lymington, Hants
and printed in Great Britain by
Richard Clay Ltd, Bungay, Suffolk

The Kingdom

It's a long way off but inside it
There are quite different things going on:
Festivals at which the poor man
Is king and the consumptive is
Healed; mirrors in which the blind look
At themselves and love looks at them
Back; and industry is for mending
The bent bones and the minds fractured
By life. It's a long way off, but to get
There takes no time and admission
Is free, if you will purge yourself
Of desire, and present yourself with
Your need only and the simple offering
Of your faith, green as a leaf.

R. S. Thomas

CONTENTS

ACKNOWLEDGMENTS

This book was shaped by several attempts to treat the same theme for different purposes and on different occasions and I wish to express my indebtedness both to those who invited me and those who gave me their attention and response at the Good Friday Three Hours Service in Westminster Abbey, the Cantess Summer School at Canterbury, and the Provincial Conference of the Scottish Episcopal Church, all in 1988, and the Clergy Residential Conferences of the dioceses of Chelmsford and Chester, both in 1989.

I am most grateful to R. S. Thomas, and to his publishers, Macmillan London Limited, for permission to use his poem, *The Kingdom*, as a frontispiece and inspiration to the whole book; also to the executors of Edwin Muir and his publishers Faber and Faber for permission to quote his poem, *The Road*.

The biblical extracts in chapters 3–6 are from the Revised Standard Version, © 1946 by the Division of Christian Education of the National Council of the Churches of Christ in the USA, with occasional modification and insertions (in brackets) of my own.

My particular thanks go to Dr Kathleen Hall, lately of Southampton University, and to Sister Margaret of the All Saints Sisters of the Poor, for typing the book.

John V. Taylor

PRELUDE

The Quest

The brief public life of Jesus of Nazareth was an explosion of energy without parallel in recorded history. At first it seemed, however intense, a very local explosion. The Jewish historian Josephus, writing in Rome fifty to sixty years later, devoted no more space to Jesus than to other leaders of short-lived movements.[1] But what Jesus started was not short-lived; even Josephus remarks that 'the tribe of the Christians, so called after him, has still to this day not disappeared'. The shock-waves of those two and a half years ran on in ever-widening circles.

No doubt this was largely due to the belief that Jesus had been raised from the dead and was still a living personal presence, active in the lives of his followers. In that belief men and women who had never known him 'in the flesh' found that his story and his teaching had the same transforming impact upon them as he had made upon people in Palestine before his death. The significance of that fact lies in the continuity. Faith in his resurrection gave a massive boost and a vast expansion to the influence Jesus had begun to exercise over the thought and will of human beings; but it was not the resurrection that started it.

The Gospel of Mark sets out specifically to make this very point. 'The beginning of the Good News of Jesus Christ, the Son of God,' was not the announcement of his rising from the dead which, initially at least, induced only fear and silence, but the voice of John the Baptist heralding Jesus'

1

entry upon his public ministry. John was the detonator of the ensuing explosion, and no other word will do to describe the onrush of power and challenge that floods the next nine chapters of this Gospel.

According to the separate traditions, Moses, Confucius and the Buddha all had a period of some forty years in which to establish a way of life among their followers. The Prophet Muhammad had twenty-two years for passing on the revelation that was bestowed through him. Yet within little more than thirty months Jesus of Nazareth proclaimed something and did something and *was* something that immediately fired the imagination of the common people, brought about a radical change of direction in many of them, and has gone on doing so ever since. Not consistently; that is all too obvious. The Christianity of all the churches has from time to time, and often, been a travesty of the mind and spirit of the Gospels. But the acknowledged way of renewal has forever been to return closer to the original inspiration and bring the authentic message of Jesus back into circulation so that it speaks to a new generation as freshly as it spoke to his contemporaries.

Though we may not understand what he meant by it, we know what the gospel of Jesus Christ was. 'The time has come; the Kingdom of God is almost here; turn your minds around and believe the good news.' Here is the keynote of the faith of Jesus of Nazareth. Here is the word which, on his lips, moved people with such extraordinary power. If we could resuscitate that declaration so that it conveyed in the terms and in the experience of our world the essence of what it meant to his, might it not stir the pulse and quicken the imagination of a new generation in our own day and restore a clarity of purpose to the churches?

ONE

The Authentic Voice

The cry 'Back to Galilee!' has almost invariably been an invitation to romantic fiction. It is dangerously easy to re-create a Jesus in our own image by the dubious methods of a historical novelist whose mediæval monks or ancient Greek heroes possess an idiom and insights conveniently like our own. Such facile similitude has little or nothing to do with the far stranger and more exacting relevance of Jesus persisting through time over the minds and hearts of people of all kinds. That captivating immediacy cannot be divorced from his message, though many have attempted to do so, since teaching, practice and person are inextricably integrated in the figure of Jesus that the Gospels present. But to identify his authentic message, to discern what Jesus meant by it, and then to envisage the terms in which that meaning might carry significance and conviction for these very different times, are three stages in a single task, and it is anything but a simple one. Not a few scholars have, in fact, concluded that it is impossible, considered both as a literary and as a historical problem. Fortunately for the spiritual life of humanity, many people can grasp truth of this kind, or rather, can be grasped by it, intuitively and without logical deduction. For such the recognition of Jesus' gospel is not a problem. It confronts them without benefit of scholars, just as it confronted late mediæval lay folk without benefit of clergy. Yet, even so, the reasoned investigations of the scholar, like the authority of the schoolman in a pre-critical

3

age, can if they do not quench faith, serve to correct and refute extravagant private interpretations and to confirm really perceptive insight. They may also throw open new aspects of the truth and offer a fresh vocabulary with which to make it clear.

What makes it difficult to establish with certainty what it was that Jesus proclaimed is the nature of the Gospels themselves. Through the inspiration of the Spirit of God, as Christians believe, they are the product, not simply of the Evangelists who compiled them, but of Christian communities which, from the earliest days of the movement, proclaimed their faith and instructed new members of the fellowship, in the different centres and in different languages, Aramaic, Hebrew and Greek. At the start they relied heavily on the testimony of eye-witnesses to create a tradition of mission preaching. This seems to have been generally built around a summary of the ministry and message of Jesus, culminating in his death and resurrection, with references to the Old Testament to present him as the fulfilment of the divine purpose.[1] What was preached was naturally incorporated into the instruction given to converts before and after their baptism, and recited as an element in their worship, and for these purposes additional anecdotes and sayings of Jesus were brought into the repertory, couched in a more explanatory and didactic style. They were also called into service to rebut the arguments of those who either opposed the new movement or perverted its message. The terse, unadorned form in which the sayings of Jesus, and the miracle stories, are cast in the first three Gospels is typical of an oral tradition worn smooth and stylized by repetition and transmission from person to person. In the New Testament Epistles there are several instances of their authors recalling this primitive oral tradition as the authority for their gospel, and using it for both teaching and controversy.[2]

Naturally some of the local repertories of sayings and stories were committed to writing. In certain centres this may have happened quite early. Among the Palestinian Jews the rabbinical preference for meticulously memorized oral transmission persisted side by side with a careful copying on scrolls like those of Qumran. Christian writers of the second century knew that local collections of the sayings of Jesus had been transcribed,[3] and there is internal evidence of this in the Gospels themselves. It followed as a matter of course that early attempts were made at some coherent and comprehensive narrative as the only means whereby a growing number of Christians could understand what they were talking about when they professed 'Jesus is Lord'. Among those early accounts Irenæus in the second century referred to a gospel written in Hebrew, allegedly by the apostle Matthew; and, though the matter remains unresolved, some of the scholars who have studied the literary relationships of the first three Gospels to each other have concluded that there must have been a previous written narrative on which they all drew.[4]

When each of the four Evangelists in turn set about compiling his Gospel in the form we possess, none of them approached the task with the objective detachment of a modern historian. Undoubtedly they were at pains to present a true account, but they were writing as believers for believers about him who was the focus of their belief, the Lord who had been raised from death; and their purpose was to endorse and strengthen that faith. Within that common purpose, moreover, each was pursuing his own specific aim. The Gospel attributed to Matthew appears to have been compiled from within, and for, a Jewish-Christian community in Galilee or Syria as a textbook presenting the teaching and the purpose of Jesus in such a way as to equip that church to maintain its identity in relation to the surrounding Judaism.[5] The compiler of the second of our Gospels gives a somewhat deceptive impres-

5

sion of having artlessly set down portions of reminiscence as they were related to him, with little attempt to write them up, apart from placing them in a chronological scheme of two parts, the first culminating at Cæsarea Philippi and the second in Jerusalem. There are indications that this material was originally intended for the instruction of candidates for baptism in a Latin-speaking church.[6]

The third Gospel was addressed to Gentiles of the imperial world to convince them that the Jesus of Palestine was central to a divine plan for all humanity. With this aim in view the author composed a much broader two-part scenario, placing the resurrection not at the end but at the centre. His two books might be titled 'Up to Jerusalem' and 'On to Rome', with an emphasis on the Holy Spirit to provide continuity. Yet he seems to have realized that, for all its originality, his theological framework would carry conviction only if it was faithful to the common tradition. So we find him both adding and omitting material, but only once changing the primitive order of events in the story; and, though he could write the most elegant Greek, he sometimes retained barbarities of style that more truly represented his sources.[7] As to the fourth Gospel, the most convincing of many conflicting views is that which recognizes in it an early Palestinian, or even Judæan, provenance which has been used in a very individual way to elicit personal faith in Jesus, especially among Hellenized and proselyte Jews, in some cosmopolitan city like Ephesus (with which it has traditionally been linked). The author presents the central figure in a selection of episodes which he dramatizes so as to bring out the interplay between Jesus and other, often named, characters – a method that has been compared with Plato's presentation of Socrates. This portrayal of Jesus is therefore the most interpretative and theological of the four Gospels, though it needs to be said that this fact is much exaggerated by critics who read into some of the sayings and comments a more fully-fledged and anachronistic doctrine than they necessarily were intended to convey.[8]

Since, then, the Gospels were formed by such processes and for such purposes, it was only natural that the words in which the narratives and sayings were reported, the significance that was given to them, and the principle on which they were selected and arranged, should all reflect the convictions and concerns of the Christians who preserved them and the authors who gave them their final shape. There are those who take the re-assuring view that in this instance what was 'only natural' did not take place, since God decided that so much was at stake it called for a supernatural providence: words and events were transmitted exactly as they occurred, and discrepancies are only apparent. But if one believes that it is God's way to entrust the greatest issues to the most natural means, it follows that no one can prove beyond question that any particular episode or saying in the Gospels happened exactly as it is reported, and has not been recast to some extent by the needs or presuppositions of those who transmitted it. To recognize this, however, by no means indicates that the historical person of Jesus is beyond the reach of our knowledge. Though we may not assert absolutely that he said this or did that, there are sound ways by which we can judge the degree of probability that the account is reliable or the words authentic; and in many instances the probability is very strong.

Consider, for example, the extent to which the earliest testimony to the teaching of Jesus may have become adapted, in the course of its transmission, to answer questions that arose in the life of the local church and its teaching of enquirers. A simple instance of this is the parable of the Lost Sheep. Because of the artistry with which the author has added two similar parables of the Lost Coin and the Lost Son, we tend to remember the version in Luke 15, where the story is told by Jesus in defence of his association with sinners and outsiders. In Matthew 18, however, the story is set in the context of a lesson on mutual care within the community of Christians. The shepherd's care for the stray sheep is an analogy of the church's pastoral care of his 'little ones' which must reflect the love of God. The next verses (Matt. 18.15–18) offer a regulatory answer to the question, 'How is this care of the erring member to be administered?', and they envisage an ecclesiastical situation very like that to which St Paul addressed his instruction in I Cor. 5.1–8. Now it is not impossible that Jesus should have looked forward to such an organizational problem among his followers, though, if that were so, it would radically modify the usual understanding of his mission, and it is in any case uncharacteristic of the Jesus of the Gospels to speak of an excommunicated member as 'a Gentile and a tax collector'. These considerations make it appear more likely that the later verses and the setting of the parable in this context were both derived from some Christian synagogue's application of the original tradition to its needs and, by the same token, that the parable, in some other context, is an authentic piece of the teaching of Jesus.

Yet, in our use of this principle of discernment, scepticism should always be moderated by remembering the extraordinary care that rabbis in the time of Jesus took to ensure that their precepts would be accurately transmitted by word of mouth. They cast their teaching in a rhythmical, easily remembered form and had their pupils repeat it until they knew it perfectly by heart. Those pupils would then be at liberty to add their own glosses and interpretations without losing the authentic core of the master's words. Many passages of teaching attributed to Jesus in the Gospels suggest that he also employed this method. Even in an English translation, the Sermon on the Mount, the parables of the Sower and of the Sheep and the Goats, or the saying about saving or losing one's life ring unforgettably in the memory. Students of Aramaic have reconstructed the probable original of many other passages of Jesus' speech and found that they fall into the same memorable rhythms.

In considering the reliability of any oral tradition of whatever period of history, it is worth noting one feature of the process of passing anecdotes round, wearing them smooth by repetition or embellishing them by imagination: while the subject may be credited with some things he never said, any idiosyncrasy or personal style of his is enshrined, even to the point of caricature. In a flippant vein one can recall the popular take-offs of Winston Churchill, Field Marshal Montgomery or Archbishop Michael Ramsay. Dr Spooner of New College may never have perpetrated a single spoonerism, yet those who knew him admitted that this form of verbal confusion encapsulated the essential oddity of the man. The Gospels contain clear traces of just such mannerisms reproduced in the telling. One that has often been noted is Jesus' peculiar use of the phrase, 'Verily I say to you,' or literally, 'Amen, I tell you.' The normal use of the Hebrew or Aramaic word 'Amen' was the same in those days as it has been ever since: it was used by others at the close of someone's speech or prayer to confirm and endorse it: 'Hear! Hear!' 'So be it.' That is how 'Amen' is used elsewhere in the New Testament. Only in the Gospels, and only from the lips of Jesus, do we hear the word used in this arresting way to introduce a statement: 'Amen, I tell you.' If the phrase occurred frequently in only one Gospel or one of the sources on which the authors drew, we might surmise that it originated in the teaching method or the liturgical recitations of a particular community. But in fact it crops up in the sayings of Jesus in every strand of which the Synoptic Gospels are compiled.[9] It does not seem to have been preserved in the tradition for any theological significance it might have carried, for there is no evidence of this being exploited in the New Testament or the Apostolic Fathers of the Church. The only two references outside the

Gospels to this remembered style of speech depend for their point on its having been a distinctive idiom of Jesus himself. In denying that there has been any vacillation in his dealings with the Christians at Corinth, Paul likens his constancy to that of Jesus Christ who 'was not Yes and No, but in him it has always been Yes. For all the promises of God find their Yes in him, so also in him the Amen to God's glory is uttered through us' (II Cor. 1.16–20). The same memory underlies, it would seem, the announcement of the message to the vacillating church of Laodicea in the vision of John in the Book of Revelation: 'The words of the Amen, the faithful and true witness, the beginning of God's creation' (Rev. 3.14; cf. Isa. 65.16).

There are other distinctive traits of style which students of the Gospel texts have tentatively claimed as traces of the authentic speech of Jesus, while recognizing that literary judgments of this sort must be partly subjective. C. F. Burney in the 1920s and J. Jeremias in the 1960s attempted persuasively to reconstruct the Aramaic original that underlies the Greek translation of sections of Jesus' teaching, and believed they could discern in the more poetical passages some rhythmical patterns that were characteristic of him.[10] More recently Bishop John Robinson drew attention to a use of scripture in argument which he believed was typical of Jesus, even if not uniquely his. Instead of quoting from the Old Testament to confirm a point of view, Jesus frequently threw out a reference as a 'poser' to pull his hearers up short and make them think again. Among the examples Robinson quotes are: 'Have you not read what David did when he was hungry?' (Matt. 12.3), 'Have you not read in the book of Moses, in the passage about the bush, how God said, I am the God of Abraham, Isaac and Jacob?' (Mark 12.26), 'Have you never read, "Out of the mouths of babes and sucklings thou hast brought perfect praise"?' (Matt. 21.16). The quotation makes the point without further elaboration. It can, of course, be argued that these are instances of the polemic of the early church communities. But exactly the same style of ironical challenge is implicit in Jesus' special handling of parables. He tells a story, not as an allegory but simply as an anecdote which makes its point, which his hearers may or may not get, leaving them to ponder its implication. This method appears to be so personal to Jesus, so indicative of his attitude to everyone, that we may fairly say that when we meet it we are hearing his authentic voice, and when we are caught up in didactic explanations of a parable or very obvious allegorical correlations – 'The reapers are the angels' – we have grounds for suspecting that the voice is the voice of other Christian teachers. They may be presenting something very similar to the meaning he intended, but they are using another method and for a different purpose.[11]

This approach to the Gospels does not in itself drive such a wedge between the thought of Jesus and the mind of the church as is often supposed. The prelude of this book referred to the ministry of Jesus as an explosion of energy, the shock-waves of which spread out in widening circles. But it is inevitable that, as any movement becomes institutionalized, even in its rudimentary beginnings, it faces new questions of discipline and organization, which it tries to answer with as much faithfulness as possible to the initial inspiration. Paul showed that he was aware of this in distinguishing what was known to be the Lord's teaching from his own attempts to work out its implications for questions that the Lord had not touched upon. He believed, as Christians have always done, that through the resurrection of Christ and the indwelling of the Spirit, the church enjoys a continuous contact with its Lord, and is not solely dependent for its guidance upon a backward reference to Jesus 'in the flesh'. Yet that confidence did not extinguish their concern to keep faith with the historic Jesus as their ultimate authority. So we find Paul wrestling with this problem of continuity in his direction of the Corinthian

11

church. 'I say this by way of concession, not by command.' 'To the married I give charge, not I but the Lord . . . To the rest I say, not the Lord . . .' 'Now concerning the unmarried I have no command of the Lord, but I give my opinion as one who by the Lord's mercy is trustworthy.' 'In this I think that I have the Spirit of God.' 'What I am saying I say not with the Lord's authority, but as a fool' (I Cor. 7.6,10,12,25,40; II Cor. 11.17). They are therefore in good company who apply to their exegesis of the Gospels the same principle of a general confidence in the judgment of the church that fostered the tradition, with a critical effort to distinguish between the mind of Jesus and the interpretations of the early Christian communities.

The parables repay with fresh understanding whoever approaches them with this kind of discrimination. The comparison of different versions of the same story often yields unexpected insights. Moreover, if Jesus did follow such an individual style in his use of parables as has been suggested, we may wonder whether the point-by-point explanations which are added to some of them were really his or originated in the Christian circles that repeated the stories. When one reads Matt. 13.18–23, for example, that question occurs quite naturally, and one then perceives that in fact the explanatory passage is not specifically attributed to Jesus either in Matt. 13.18 or in Mark 4.14.

Again, in view of the intense interest those circles of Jewish Christians showed in finding passages in the Old Testament scriptures that seemed to be descriptive of Jesus or fulfilled by him, it would be natural for them, when retelling the narratives, to lay added stress on such correlations, even to the point of adjusting the story to fit. It has often been pointed out that almost every detail in Mark's account of the crucifixion which was possibly based on an earlier passion story used by all the Synoptic Gospels, can be coupled with some verse in the Old Testament. But while we may freely admit that a fact and its religious significance are prone to be confused, this is no warrant for dismissing as fiction every episode that seems to re-enact an Old Testament phrase. There is enough in the Old Testament to match a multitude of natural events! So the verse in Psalm 22, for example – 'They part my garments among them, and upon my vesture they cast lots' – may properly alert a reader of Mark's Gospel to the possibility that it gave rise to that episode of the crucifixion story, or at least influenced its details. But before jumping to that conclusion, the reader should also recall that it was customary for the executioners to keep the clothes of the condemned, so the event would have happened anyway. Discernment comes to those who keep an open mind, weigh the probabilities in each case, and are patient with uncertainty.

Once it is recognized that, in spite of the phenomenal fidelity of oral transmission, the original testimony to the teaching and actions of Jesus may in some instances have been slanted to fit the later preoccupations and questions of the developing Christian communities that were using it, another rough and ready criterion emerges to help towards identifying such adaptations. It has been called the similarity principle. Where some element in a Gospel corresponds closely to a theme or a matter of concern which we know, from elsewhere in the New Testament or other sources, was prominent in the early Christian churches, this may indicate that the churches' interest has shaped that passage in the Gospel; and, conversely, a theme in the Gospels that does not feature very frequently in the rest of the New Testament is the more likely to be authentic. To take one example, a theme which stands out in the Epistles to the Galatians and the Romans is the lack of response to the gospel by Jews of the Dispersion, and the efforts of Christian Judaizers to lay the full burden of the Jewish ritual regulations upon Christian converts. It may well be that the anxiety and acrimony of these relationships 'rubbed off' in the retelling of Jesus' encounters

13

with the Pharisees of his day and his diatribes against them and the jurists (Matt. 23.4–36).

Yet, although the logic of this criterion is convincing, it proves quite difficult in practice to find examples that do not turn around and lead to an opposite conclusion. The question of a Christian's freedom to eat 'unclean' foods which in one form or another troubled the churches both at Corinth and at Rome might, on the principle of similarity, cast some doubt upon the authenticity of the words ascribed to Jesus in Mark 7.14–23 and Matt. 15.10–20: 'Not what goes into the mouth defiles a man, but what comes out of the mouth, this defiles a man.' This doubt is made stronger by the inclusion at the end of this passage of a catalogue of sins or virtues that is more typical of the Epistles than the Gospels. Yet in Paul's treatment of the matter in Rom. 14.13–17 there are indications that, as elsewhere, he is invoking as his authority an oral tradition of the actual words of Jesus: 'I know and am persuaded *in the Lord Jesus* that nothing is unclean in itself.' He also includes the injunction not to judge, and he refers, uncharacteristically, to the Kingdom of God. So it could be argued that he is very deliberately harking back to an authentic tradition of Jesus' words and transposing them to this problem of the Gentile church – if, indeed, the church in Rome was predominantly Gentile at that time. That points to a further weakness in the similarity principle. It is clear that the source material of the Synoptic Gospels has come mainly from Jewish-Christian communities in or near to Palestine, and there is very little independent material that tells what questions were troubling them. This has to be largely surmised from the Gospels, so the argument is circular. For example, it has been argued that, because the text of the account of the healing of the paralytic in Mark 2.1–12 is notoriously hard to read aloud without giving a dramatic performance – 'then said he to the paralytic' – the whole section of six verses about the forgiveness of the man's sins may be an interpolation that

14

originated from the defence that Christians advanced when Jewish neighbours said that their claim to forgive sins in the name of Jesus was blasphemous. But, while it is plausible enough to say that those neighbours found the Christian claim offensive, there is no evidence of the fact; it is surmised from the Gospel account, which may, after all, be a coherent reproduction of a dramatic rendering of the actual event.

This, perhaps, is one reason why more recent analysis of the Gospel material has concentrated afresh on a much earlier interest, namely the more demonstrable contrast between one Evangelist's handiwork and another's. His final choice and arrangement of the material indicates each compiler's conception and aim, and this, in turn, enables the reader to discern with more likelihood which passages are that compiler's own comment, and where his hand has been at work. From this process, too, the outline of the original, and much of the characteristic detail, emerge more certainly.

So, reverting to the subject of this book, it is possible to discern a difference of emphasis in the interpretations that the Gospels of Matthew and Luke give to the message of Jesus about the Kingdom of God, and, by taking this into account, possible to arrive at a clearer understanding of the authentic and uniquely novel message itself. All the Synoptists assert that, however understood, the Kingdom of God was his dominant theme. The expression occurs with remarkable frequency in the teaching they ascribe to Jesus – forty-eight times in Matthew, fifteen in Mark and forty-five in Luke-Acts. As there are only twenty-four references to the Kingdom in the rest of the New Testament, it cannot be regarded as a preoccupation of the Christian communities of later decades which they transposed back into the mouth of Jesus. Moreover, such evidence as exists indicates that the expression 'the Kingdom of God' was used much less frequently in the rabbinic literature of the period than it was in the teaching of Jesus. It must have been, therefore, the very keynote of the faith of Jesus himself, and to understand what it meant to him is, arguably, the primary task of any who claim to be his followers.

TWO

Expectation in the Air

The manifesto with which Jesus launched his Galilean mission is summed up in the words: 'The Kingdom of God is close at hand. Turn about and believe it.' And from among those who responded he appears quite soon to have chosen some to go around announcing the same declaration. Whether or not John the Baptist had included this Kingdom theme in his preaching, as the Gospel of Matthew alone asserts, it seems clear that such a proclamation could be made without a preamble to explain it. In other words, the Kingdom of God was already a familiar idea among the Jews of that time, so that a public speaker who used the phrase could take it for granted that most of his hearers would know what he was talking about.

The actual words that Jesus used in Aramaic, the common language of the area, were probably *malkuta dishemaya*, which literally mean 'kingdom of the heavens'. That did not, however, signify the 'Heaven' of later Christian hymns or visions of the after-life. 'The heavens' is simply one of the substitute phrases that devout Jews preferred to use instead of naming God directly, similar to 'the Most High', or 'the Lord', or even 'the Place'. So the Gospel of Matthew, reflecting its Jewish-Christian background, makes great use of the idiomatic 'Kingdom of Heaven', while Mark and Luke give the intended meaning of the phrase, which is 'Kingdom, or reign, of God'.

The idea of God's reign was rooted in the very beginnings

of Jewish religion and in the formative experience out of which that religion was born. 'I am Yahweh, your God, who brought you out of the land of Egypt.' No matter how small-scale that escape may have been – and the pre-history of the Hebrew tribes and their entry into the land of Palestine is a fascinating, but complicated study – the memory of it became one of the most compelling symbols not only for the Jewish race but for oppressed people everywhere. The thought that God, out of his compassion and grace, had identified himself with the fortunes of one such group, had rescued them, given them a homeland and made them his own people, created an altogether new concept of human destiny and responsibility under God. The germ of the ideal of the Kingship of God lay in that memory. The other gods of that ancient world were local manifestations of the universal powers of nature, sun and moon, storm and fertility, and so on. But this God of the Hebrews was not equated with any such life-force; he had made himself known in that historical event. The local Baal, as the word signifies, was the Owner of his portion of *land* and demanded the inhabitants' tribute. Yahweh was the Lord, or Ruler, of his *people*, concerned for what they did and what befell them, sharing himself with them and demanding their obedience to his laws. 'The problem of life was seen, not as an integration with the forces of nature, but as an adjustment to the will of the God who had chosen them.'[1]

One might say, therefore, that they began to live with a dream of God's reign: God in their midst as champion-protector, and his people responding with obedience to his will. In the early days their understanding of this God's nature was no doubt limited largely to the observance of tabus and prohibitions and the fortunes of war. The Book of Judges gives a fair picture of the spiritual values of those times. There was need for much development and refinement as their history unfolded. Yet from the start they seem to have recognized three strands in the demand that their relationship with Yahweh laid upon them: theological, ritual and moral. The basic theological demand was that he alone must be their God, never imaged or represented in any physical form. It was an exacting standard for them in what we would describe today as a pluralist society, and they frequently fell short of the demand. Yet, while archæologists have unearthed innumerable figurines of female deities among Israelite debris, scarcely any male representations of a god have come to light. To that extent the dream kingdom kept its hold on them.

The ritual laws necessarily reflected the cultural changes and political vicissitudes through which the nation passed, and no doubt liturgical development was as contentious among their priests and jurists as it continues to be for our own. Yet circumcision and the sabbath and certain tabus and seasonal festivals seem to have remained constant symbols of their identity as the people of Yahweh.

But what most distinguished them from the surrounding nations was the social morality which their God expected as a reciprocal response to his past goodness towards them, and a condition of his abiding presence. Though they never stated it in precisely these terms, it would not be far from the truth to say that the God who can not be imagined in any physical form was calling for a reflection of his likeness within the social life of the people he had made his own. The historians of Israel, even in their earliest accounts, used the word *chesed* (pronounced with an initial gutteral ch, as in the Scots loch), which means merciful fidelity or faithful love, to denote God's special grace towards the Hebrew people; and they found in every human demonstration of *chesed* that imitation of the divine activity which God was looking for. So, following the death of Saul, David honours the men of Jabesh-Gilead with the words: 'May you be blessed by Yahweh, because you showed this faithful love to Saul your lord, and buried him. Now may Yahweh show faithful love and steadfastness to you' (II Sam. 2.5,6). Again, David's merciful treatment of the family of Jonathan is actually called 'the *chesed* of God' (I Sam. 20.14; II Sam. 9.3). It was, however, the eighth-century prophets, and the Deuteronomic school of writing that followed them in the next hundred years, who brought to the fore this way of looking at the moral demands of Yahweh as a reciprocation of his treatment of his people. 'He has showed you, O man, what is good; and what does Yahweh require of you but to act justly, and to love merciful fidelity, and to walk humbly with your God?' (Micah 6.8). The imitation of God's faithful love, 'doing as you have been done by', is the quintessence of obedience to God's rule. The poor of the land are to be shown kindness – 'for you shall remember that you were a slave in the land of Egypt, and Yahweh your God redeemed you.' The same recollection is given as the ground for letting the widows and orphans, slaves and aliens, glean the fields and orchards, never denying them justice, and including them in the hospitality of the great national festivals (Deut. 15.15; 16.11–12; 24.17–22; Lev. 25.37–38).[2] That reforming school of thought tried also to turn the nation's ritual obedience and religious celebrations into acts of recollection, re-enacting the past in such a way as to bring it into present experience and make it the worshippers' own story, so that their conduct might better reflect the ways of their God with his people (Deut. 5.14–15; 16.3; 24.8,9).

Even before the Deuteronomic movement, the Kingship of Yahweh was a theme ritually reiterated in the Temple worship. There is general agreement, in spite of some past exaggerations, that many of the psalms seem, in their present form, to have been adapted for use in some kind of dramatic recitation or liturgical representation of Yahweh's victory over his enemies and triumphant enthronement.

Lift up your heads, O you gates, and be lifted up, you everlasting doors, and the King of glory shall come in.

Who is the King of glory? the Lord of hosts, he is the King of glory (Ps. 24.9,10).

God has gone up with the sound of rejoicing, and Yahweh to the blast of the ram's horn.
O sing praises, sing praises to God, O sing praises, sing praises to our King.
God has become the King of all nations, he has taken his seat upon his holy throne (Ps. 47.5,6,8).

The accounts of King Saul's election (I Sam. 8–12) show that there were two views as to whether the human monarchy threatened or strengthened the people's sense of God's Kingship over them. But there can be no doubt that the reign of David, and the belief that God had promised an unending succession to his dynasty, became almost as potent a symbol as the Exodus in the later development of Judaism. By establishing his capital in the recently captured Jerusalem, unifying the nation and making plans to build the Temple, he bequeathed to his people for all time an unfading vision of the Kingdom of God, the Holy City and the Messiah King, which persisted through all the disillusionments that the abuse of monarchy brought to the succeeding generations.[3]

The actualization of God's rule was an impossible ideal for human society, yet the Jews could not abandon it without repudiating their relationship with him. Their evident failure induced guilt as well as disappointment. Each political disaster, and every period of lifelessness in their religion, were taken to be God's chastisement to bring his people back to obedience and blessing. Consistently, from the capture of the Ark by the Philistines to the captivity of the Jews in Babylonia, the penalty they most dreaded was his withdrawal from the nation. But just as they could not reject his rule over them without losing their cultural identity, neither could Yahweh disown his people without abrogating that faithful love which is the essence of his being.

> How can I give you up, Ephraim, how surrender you,
> Israel? . . .
> I will not turn about and destroy Ephraim, for I am God
> and not a man, the Holy One in your midst (Hos. 11.8,9).

Judgment there must be, 'the Day of Yahweh', as it was called, bringing an evil dynasty or corrupt era to an end in order to make a new start possible; but Yahweh will never abandon his people. His forgiveness is a foregone conclusion. It is there at all times, awaiting only their turning back to the former relationship and to the unchanging purpose of establishing his kingship in their midst. 'Return to me, and I will return to you, says the Lord of hosts' (Mal. 3.7).

It was judgment, in fact, the actual destruction of the kingdom, that brought about a great blossoming of the idea of the Kingdom of God. There were three distinct elements in the change, all prompted by the radical alteration in the circumstances in which the exiles found themselves. Detached from their own land, yet knowing Yahweh to be still accessible, their concept of his rule became universal. He who had been their Lord by virtue of his having delivered them was seen to be King of the whole earth by virtue of having created it, and they visualized that act of creation as a cosmic replica of their own redemption from darkness and chaos. Now they saw that his purpose of establishing his rule over them as a special people was a means towards the fuller realization of his kingship and his presence in all the world.

At the same time their concept of obedience to God's rule became more codified. All the social interactions and responsibilities of agricultural or city life had vanished. When rich and poor were reduced to a common deportee status, how were any of them to live out the merciful kindness of Yahweh? It was simpler to prescribe the will of

God in regulations derived from the older directions, and, by the nature of such things, rituals and prohibitions proved more amenable to codification than justice and faithful love. A new style of spirituality resulted, based upon veneration of the Torah and devout individual observance as the way to secure God's sovereignty over every detail of life.

The third element in the change that the exile of the Jews brought about was a zoom-lens shift of focus in the hope that was to inspire the Jewish people after the exile. At first the expectations of some of them were immediate enough. The greatest of their prophets were depicting in superb poetry their imminent restoration to their own land. In the event, however, many did not return. Those who did so were the Zionists of their day, enabling all Jews to recognize that they were a nation once more with a homeland of their own, even while exile remained their permanent condition. In any case, those who had come back to the land and built the second temple enjoyed only a limited independence, with no occupant on the throne of David. Yet the resounding prophecies of judgment and destruction combined with the lyrical visions of restoration to demand some more perfect fulfilment. So they began to look beyond the present era of history to some ultimate 'Day of Yahweh' by which God would sweep away the *status quo* to make way for a new period for the world in which his presence and his sovereignty would be fully realized.

This projection of the promised Reign of God into a future that lies beyond some catastrophic ending of the present state of affairs is given the name 'eschatology', after the Greek word *eschaton*, 'last'. It is a mistake to read into all the eschatological hopes of the biblical writers the later Christian idea of a heavenly after-life on a non-temporal plane. The Kingdom of God is not heaven; it is God's rule perfectly realized in a new age upon this earth. It is the old dream of right relationships come true through the action of God alone. There was as much diversity of opinion about the part that a Messiah was to play in these hopes as there had been about the role of the king in God's purpose for his people; but the inclusion of a Messiah in their vision of the new age was a further factor anchoring it firmly to the sphere of temporal existence. The eschatological view of the Kingdom of God grew quite independently of any belief in life after death. It was the remnant who survived the final catastrophe who were to become the germ of the new future (Ezek. 4.1–12; Joel 2.28–32; Zeph. 3.8–10; Zech. 9.9–10; 14).

It was one thing to recall such scriptures, but quite another thing to interpret their meaning. The Jews who drifted back to their own land from time to time after their exile might well have asked, like the Ethiopian eunuch long after, 'Of whom is the prophet speaking here? Of himself and his own day, or of others and some other time?' The expectations which those past visions inspired in the minds of the Jewish contemporaries of Jesus were as varied as are the future hopes of Christians today, or for that matter the hopes of world Jewry today.

It was about 170 years before the birth of Jesus that Jewish speculations about God's ultimate purpose for their race assumed a new intensity and began to crystalize into opposing schools of thought. At that time many of the aristocratic families associated with the hereditary high priests were strongly drawn to the rationalism and the luxurious life-style of the Greek culture that had surrounded them since Alexander's conquest of the Levant, and they were prepared to go to almost any lengths to 'liberalize', as they saw it, the religion and customs of their people. The Seleucid ruler of the whole region, Antiochus Epiphanes, took advantage of their collusion to forward his own policy of destroying Judaism. In resistance to this idea there was a strong movement of *Chasidim*, or 'faithful ones', those who have *chesed*, dedicated to the purity of Judaism and its eventual independence. To this movement we should ascribe the symbolic visions of the Book of Daniel. 'In the period of those kings the God of heaven will establish a kingdom which shall never be destroyed; that kingdom shall never pass to another people; it shall shatter and make an end of all these kingdoms, while it shall itself endure for ever' (Dan. 2.44). A little later, during the revolution led by Judas Maccabeus and his family, who were named Hasmonæans after an ancestor, the visions of the Book of Daniel become more specific. 'I saw one like a son of man coming with the clouds of heaven; he approached the Ancient in Years and was presented to him. Sovereignty and glory and kingly power were given to him so that all people and nations of every language should serve him; his sovereignty was to be an everlasting sovereignty which should not pass away' (Dan. 7.13,14).

The *Chasidim*, however, included many who were not at ease in the political struggle. They were the heirs of that religious movement which came to birth through the experience of the Exile, concerned to raise up a holy people, securing God's rule over themselves through strict observance of his law. That, they believed, was the limit of what human effort could achieve, and on such a people God would, by his own intervention in history, confer the promised kingdom. The visions in the Book of Daniel continue, therefore, with this promise: 'The kingly power, sovereignty and greatness of all the kingdoms under heaven shall be given to the people of the holy ones of the Most High. Their kingly power is an everlasting power, and all sovereignties shall serve them and obey them' (Dan. 7.27).

The subsequent history of the Hasmonæan dynasty after the victory of their revolution fulfilled the worst fears of the *Chasidim*. Simon, the brother of Judas Maccabeus, who assumed the High Priesthood for himself and his heirs, became primarily the secular ruler of a newly independent state, entering into an alliance with Rome and maintaining an army of foreign troops. When his son, John Hyrcanus, succeeded him as High Priest in 135 BC the *Chasidim* broke decisively from the Hasmonæan nobility.

The aristocratic Hellenizers, on the other hand, having recognized the invincible resistance of the national religion, accommodated themselves to the new order and became the chief supporters of the Hasmonæans. They were supremely interested in preserving the independence of the State. They still admired the urbane rationalism of Greek culture and were lax over Jewish exclusiveness. The book Ecclesiasticus is typical of their prudent wisdom at its best. Observance of the Torah became for them the outward symbol and guarantee of the nation's identity, demanding exact formal obedience, especially with regard to the temple offerings, but no supplementation or up-dating.

From these developments in the middle of the second century before Christ grew three of the religious parties that were active in the time of Jesus, each with their different preoccupations and expectations. From the *Chasidim* came the Pharisees, a largely lay movement organized in local fellowships, or synagogues, as they called them. Hence it appears that one of the names by which they were known was *Chaberim*, or Companions. The prime concern of the Pharisee movement was to recall their fellow Jews to a perfect observance of the Torah so that God might enter upon his royal rule over his holy nation in the sight of all. They held that since God had revealed his will for them in the Torah, it must be within the reach of ordinary people to follow its precepts fully, even in the very changed circumstances of their own day. So with the professional help of their jurists, those Scribes who belonged to the movement, they set about interpreting the injunctions of a more primitive period in terms that, however hard, could be fulfilled practically. They built up a body of legal opinions on every conceivable question, a system of casuistry called *halakhah*, or traditions, to which they ascribed an authority equal to that of the Torah itself. Their interest in interpreting and adapting the scriptures encouraged them to speculate on matters concerning which the scriptures themselves were silent or non-committal. So it came about that the Pharisees developed a positive doctrine of a future resurrection of the body, a final judgment, and a belief in spirits and angels. This expository function was so central to the aims of the movement that, although the Pharisee fellowship groups were intended for pious lay people, the professional jurists came to be seen as their leaders and representatives. So another name for the Pharisees was *Chakamim*, or Sages, and it was undoubtedly this element in the Pharisee movement that, surviving the destruction of the Temple in AD 70, flowed on as the mainstream of rabbinic Judaism. It is not surprising that this manifestation of Pharisaism won the general esteem of the people of the land, as Josephus frequently affirms.[4] The sincerity of their piety, their evident concern to make religion accessible to ordinary people, and their generous almsgiving and works of charity, all contributed to this popularity.

But part of the Pharisee movement must have developed in a more negative direction. Throughout the history of religion those who have formed regulated groups for the pursuit of more scrupulous standards have been tempted to become exclusive and self-righteous, and it would be extraordinary if some of the Pharisee fellowships had not followed that tendency. We know, in fact, from other sources than the Gospels, that some of the *Chaberim* Companions wanted to apply the priestly rules of ritual purity to their own lay members.[5] This entailed strict avoidance of many kinds of contamination, including social and business relationships with the common people. Thus there arose a conflict between two types which almost amounted to an inherent contradiction within Pharisaism itself. Starting from a vision of holiness as something possible for all, some of them ended with a narrow scrupulosity that entailed withdrawal from all but a few. The contradiction is embodied in the very word *perushim*, from which the name Pharisees may have been derived. It means 'the separated ones' and, like our word 'saint', can be a term of approbation. But in rabbinic literature it is more often than not used to denote a harmful excess of separatism. The Gospel traditions are mistaken in tarring all Pharisees with the same brush. But that there were such censorious groups as the Gospels describe, rightly or wrongly, as Pharisees, is a fact well supported by the evidence.[6]

An even more extreme development from the earlier *Chasidim* was the Essene monastic movement. When first one and then another of the brothers of Judas Maccabeus combined the roles of war-lord and High Priest, the Essenes repudiated the whole Jerusalem priesthood and determined to offer instead the sacrifices of ascetic holiness. They retired from the world into monastic communities, either in the rural villages or in the desert. They shared their goods in common, practised celibacy and submitted to the rule of a harsh, four-tier hierarchy and a strict routine of prayer, study and labour. They carried Sabbath observance to extreme lengths. Yet they were noted for a gentle care for people in need, and they abjured the use of slaves. Their daily life was marked by several ritual washings and a fraternal meal for all members. They believed that they alone were 'the elect of the new covenant', the sons of light who were in conflict with the sons of darkness; they therefore loved those whom God loved and hated those whom God hated. They trusted that, if they remained loyal to their chosen way and to their founder, the Teacher of Righteousness, God would eventually send them two Messiahs, one military and one priestly, when they would play their part in a final war of liberation. The Qumran community is for us the best known of the many Essene fraternities.

In sharp contrast to these two offshoots from the *Chasidim*, the Sadducees were the successors of the priestly nobility. Their status and wealth depended on the Temple services and on the position of the High Priest as head of the Jewish people. Their over-riding interest was to maintain the nation-state with as much independence as they could wheedle out of Rome. The pursuit of this policy brought them into an uneasy alliance with the Herodian dynasty and its supporters. They inherited the old taste for Greek culture and foreign contacts, but regarded a rigid adherence to the Torah as necessary for the survival of their national identity. So they clung to a literal adherence to its regulations, even in penal matters, and strongly objected to all innovations or adaptations, including belief in resurrection or supernatural powers. 'Who will sing praises to the Most High in Hades as those who are alive give thanks?' asks the Sadducee author of Ecclesiasticus. 'From the dead, as one who does not exist, thanksgiving has ceased. It is he who is alive and well who sings the Lord's praises.' So the Sadducees were not much given to other-worldly hopes, and their aspirations for this world were passionately conservative.

There was one other movement active in the lifetime of Jesus whose expectations were to affect his own destiny, and that of the whole nation. They were the revolutionaries, or 'Zealots' as they came to be called. Another name by which they were known was the *Sicarii*, or Assassins, because the members of some of their bands had sworn to eliminate any collaborator with the Roman over-rule. Though the Maccabean revolt might well have been their inspiration, the Zealots did not actually become a permanent feature in the scene until the year AD 6, when Judas of Gamara stirred up an insurrection against the census. There was a strongly religious motivation to their resistance movement, as is evident in its tragic climax at Masada. The rebels expected a political Messiah, and hoped to see the priestly Utopia prophesied by Ezekiel, though they detested the Sadducee dynasty. They also cherished expectations of miraculous intervention on behalf of their cause. Theudas (Acts 5.36), according to Josephus' garbled account, promised his followers that he would part the waters of the Jordan like another Joshua; and the rebel leader called 'The Egyptian' (Acts 21.38) was reputed to have boasted that the wall of Jerusalem would fall down before him as he advanced against the Roman troops. Wild rumour attended all these revolutionary leaders, so that in every case Josephus and the Acts of the Apostles make contradictory references to them. Jesus himself seems to have been well aware of this characteristic, for he warned: 'If anyone says to you, "Look, here is the Messiah", or "There he is", do not believe it. Imposters will come claiming to be Messiahs or prophets, and they will produce great signs and wonders to mislead even God's chosen, if such a thing were possible' (Matt. 24.23,24).

These four distinct parties among the Jews of Palestine, with their conflicting religious expectations, dominated the situation into which Jesus of Nazareth came preaching the Kingdom of God. Before considering where he stood in relation to each of them, we should stop to ask whether the question can have any relevance today. Is not this history of ideas too remote to have the slightest bearing on twentieth-century religion, or on the response which people may still make to Jesus Christ?

Looked at in detail, the beliefs and practice of those different groups are far removed from modern thought, almost to the point of incomprehension. Yet when the broad principles that they represented are discerned, it has to be said that all four of those parties are alive and well within the Christian churches of our day. The Sadducees would readily recognize those who, as much on aesthetic as on theological grounds, cherish with particular vehemence the establishment of their church as part of the national constitution and, with it, the older versions of scripture and liturgy as originally authorized. With them the survival of cultural identity is paramount. The Pharisees would appreciate the essential other-worldliness of a great deal of traditional Christianity which sees its mission primarily as saving and sanctifying souls for the world to come; and they would feel particularly at home in those church circles that foster scrupulosity of one sort or another as the path to spiritual growth. Members of the Essene communities would sympathize with the many minority groups in today's church who, having found some better way, of whatever kind, pursue it in exclusive commitment with others of like mind, and experience in their fellowship a supportive warmth that convinces them that they have the truth. And Zealots would gravitate towards the political activists who have seen the root of evil in unjust structures of power, and hold that salvation must include its eradication in the name of Christ.

In one direction or another the church of our day could have been accepted into the main religious movements in first-century Palestine. It was Jesus who did not fit in.

INTERLUDE

Where does he Stand

Where, then, did Jesus of Nazareth stand in relation to the main religious parties among the Palestinian Jews of his day? And where did each of these four groups think that he stood? Even more significantly for the long term future, what did the ever-watchful Roman authorities make of him? If those questions perplexed and eluded his contemporaries, they have been a riddle ever since to Christian and Jewish historians. Some have concluded that Jesus was recognizably a teacher of the Pharisee party, albeit with a certain laxity in his attitude to sin and ritual defilement.[1] Others have fastened on the resemblances between his ideas and the tenets of the Essene community at Qumran.[2] And there are those who point to his incriminating inclusion among the twelve apostles of certainly one member of the Zealots, and possibly more – 'Iscariot' sounds very like 'Sicarios' – and suggest that there may have been more substantial grounds than the Gospels admit for the political charge on which Jesus was condemned.[3]

All four Gospels depict a situation so tense that it was necessary for each religious party or political group to deploy discreet informers to check up on anyone with a popular following, and this is almost certainly an accurate picture of how things were.[4] The difficulty that his contemporaries found in placing Jesus is an important factor for our own attempt to understand his teaching. The following exercise may convey something of the atmosphere of universal nervous scrutiny within which Jesus preached his message of the Kingdom. Imagine reports of the words and actions of Jesus filtering through, one by one, to the leaders of each of the four main religious parties. They cannot be certain in every case whether the report is authentic or merely hearsay among the man's followers, but even rumour is indicative, so they must take them all into account. Recalling the characteristics of the four parties as described on pp.26–30, assess the impression that every reported saying or action in turn would have made upon each of the parties and place the appropriate mark in each column (preferably on a sheet of paper rather than in the book!). In each case choose one of these five 'scores':

'Sounds like one of us'	2 ticks
'For us rather than against'	1 tick
'Harmless and of no consequence'	No mark
'Not helpful to our cause'	1 cross
'An obvious opponent'	2 crosses

When you have entered a score under each party for every report, add up the four totals, counting plus 1 for every tick and minus 1 for every cross, to obtain the verdicts of the four parties.

REPORTED SAYINGS	Pharisees	Essenes	Sadducees	Zealots
1 'Unless your righteousness exceeds that of the scribes and pharisees you will never enter the Kingdom of Heaven.'				
2 'Render to Caesar the things that are Caesar's, and to God the things that are God's.'				
3 'The Sabbath was made for man, not man for the Sabbath.'				
4 'Whoever relaxes one of the least of these commandments, and teaches people so,				

34

shall be called least in the Kingdom of Heaven.'

5 'Woe to you teachers of the Law! You load people with intolerable burdens, yet you will not lift a finger to help them carry the load.'

6 'The kings of the Gentiles exercise lordship over them, and those in authority over them are called benefactors. But not so with you.'

7 'You who have followed me will also sit upon twelve thrones judging the twelve tribes of Israel.'

8 'It is easier for a camel to go through a needle's eye than for a rich man to enter the Kingdom of God.'

9 'Do you see these great buildings (the Temple)? There will not be left one stone upon another that will not be thrown down.'

10 'No one puts new wine into old wineskins; if he does, the wine will burst the skins; the wine is lost, and so are the skins.'

11 'Do not resist one who is evil. But if anyone strikes you on the right cheek, turn to him the other also.'

12 'You have heard that it was said, "You shall love your neighbour and hate your enemy". But I say to you, "Love your enemies".'

13 'I came to cast fire on the earth; and would that it were already kindled.'

14 'Blessed are you poor, for yours is the Kingdom of God.'

15 'The Kingdom of God will be taken away from you and given to a nation producing the fruits of it.'

16 'From the days of John the Baptist until
now, the Kingdom of Heaven has suffered
violence, and men of violence take it by
force.'

17 'Not what goes into the mouth defiles a
man, but what comes out of the mouth,
this defiles a man.'

18 'For your hardness of heart Moses allowed
you to divorce your wives, but from the
beginning it was not so.'

19 'As for the dead being raised . . . he is not
God of the dead but of the living; you are
quite wrong.'

20 'Let him that has no sword sell his mantle
and buy one.'

21 'Go nowhere among the Gentiles and
enter no town of the Samaritans.'

22 'The tax collectors and the harlots go into
the Kingdom of God before you.'

23 'You have a fine way of rejecting the
commandments of God in order to keep
your traditions!'

24 'Many will come from east and west and
sit at table with Abraham, Isaac and Jacob
in the Kingdom of Heaven, while the
children of the Kingdom will be thrown
into outer darkness.'

25 'Put your sword back into its place. All
who take the sword will perish by the
sword.'

26 'Beware of the leaven of the Pharisees and
the leaven of Herod.'

27 'If anyone comes to me and does not hate
his own father and mother and wife and
children and brother and sisters, yes, and
even his own life, he cannot be my disciple.'

28 'There are enuchs who have made themselves eunuchs for the sake of the Kingdom of Heaven. He who is able to receive
this, let him receive it.'

REPORTS OF ACTION

29 As he sat at table in the house many tax
collectors and sinners were sitting with
Jesus and his disciples.

30 He went on through cities and villages
and the twelve were with him, and also
some women who had been healed of evil
spirits and infirmities.

31 He called his disciples and chose from
them twelve, whom he named apostles;
Simon whom he named Peter . . . and
Simon who was called the Zealot, and
Judas the son of James, and Judas Iscariot.

32 Some Pharisees came and said to him,
'Get away from here, for Herod wants to
kill you.'

33 He strictly charged the disciples to tell no
one that he was the Messiah.

34 When Jesus saw their faith, he said to the
paralytic, 'Son, your sins are forgiven.'

35 He entered the temple and began to drive
out those who sold and bought in the
temple and overturned the tables of the
money-changers.

THREE

How Soon is Quickly?

20 *Being asked by the Pharisees when the kingdom of God was coming, he answered them, 'The kingdom of God is not coming with signs to be observed;* [21] *nor will they say, "Look, here!" or "Look, there!" for look, the kingdom of God is in the midst of you.'*

22 *And he said to the disciples, 'The days are coming when you will desire to see one of the days of the Son of man, and you will not see it.* [23] *And they will say to you, "Look, there!" or "Look, here!" Do not go, do not follow them (join that chase).* [24] *For as the lightning flashes and lights up the sky from one side to the other, so will the Son of man be in his day.* [25] *But first he must suffer many things and be rejected by this generation.* [26] *As it was in the days of Noah, so will it be in the days of the Son of man.* [27] *They ate, they drank, they married, they were given in marriage, until the day when Noah entered the ark, and the flood came and destroyed them all.* [28] *Likewise as it was in the days of Lot – they ate, they drank, they bought, they sold, they planted, they built,* [29] *but on the day when Lot went out from Sodom fire and brimstone rained from heaven and destroyed them all –* [30] *so will it be on the day when the Son of man is revealed.* [31] *On that day, let him who is on the housetop, with his goods in the house, not come down to take them away; and likewise let him who is in the field not turn back.* [32] *Remember Lot's wife.* [33] *Whoever seeks to gain his life will lose it, but whoever loses his life will preserve it.* [34] *I tell you, in that night there will be two in one bed; one will be taken and the other left.* [35] *There will be two women grinding together; one will be taken and the other left.'* [37] *And they said to him, 'Where, Lord?' He said to them, 'Where the body is, there the eagles (vultures) will be gathered together.'*

And he told them a parable, to the effect that they ought always to pray and not lose heart. [2] *He said, 'In a certain city there was a judge who neither feared God nor regarded man;* [3] *and there was a widow in*

that city who kept coming to him and saying, "Vindicate me against
my adversary." [4]For a while he refused; but afterward he said to
himself, "Though I neither fear God nor regard man, [5]yet because this
widow bothers me, I will vindicate her, or she will wear me out (shatter
me) by her continual coming."' [6]And the Lord said, 'Hear what the
unrighteous judge says. [7]And will not God vindicate his elect, who cry
to him day and night? Will he delay long over them? (Will he too put
off passing judgment in their favour?) [8]I tell you, he will vindicate
them speedily. Nevertheless, when the Son of man comes, will he find
faith on earth?'

9 He also told this parable to some who trusted in themselves that
they were righteous and despised others: [10]'Two men went up into the
temple to pray, one a Pharisee and the other a tax collector. [11]The
Pharisee stood and prayed thus with himself, "God, I thank thee that I
am not like other men, extortioners, unjust, adulterers, or even like
this tax collector. [12]I fast twice a week, I give tithes of all that I get."
[13]But the tax collecter, standing far off, would not even lift up his eyes
to heaven, but beat his breast, saying, "God, be merciful to me a
sinner!" [14]I tell you, this man went down to his house justified (as a
righteous man) rather than the other; for every one who exalts himself
will be humbled but he who humbles himself will be exalted.'

Luke 17.20–18.14

We have now taken account of the religious and political
aspirations of the four main power groups among the
Palestinian Jews in the days of Jesus, and their reaction to
him. We might have added also the Herodians – courtiers,
civil servants, military personnel and supporters, who saw
in the pretensions and the diplomacy of the Idumæan
dynasty of Herod the Great and his successors their best
hope of restoring a national kingdom. They, like the
Sadducee high priests, wanted no Messiah to unbalance the
precarious compromise with Rome. But we have so far paid
no attention to the mass of the population who belonged to
none of these parties, but for whom the hope of the
Kingdom of God was a matter of despairing urgency. The
'amme ha-arets, the people of the land, as they were called,

were pitifully poor and over-burdened. Successive campaigns had caused soaring inflation. Famine was frequent and brought extreme hardship to many of the people. Herod the Great's extravagant building and engineering projects had bled the country, and his successors did little to mitigate this extortion. On every commodity taxes were exacted, first by the Roman occupation, then by the local ruler – Herod Antipas in the case of Galilee – and, after that, by the custodians of the Temple. The normal wage of a day labourer was one denarius per day. It has been estimated that between forty and fifty per cent of a family's income was taken in taxation. The statutory ration of grain, reckoned as one and a quarter lbs. per day, cost one-twelfth of a denarius for each member of the family. The loss of a day's work, therefore, could be a serious blow. Instances of bribery mentioned in the New Testament point to a degree of corruption that must have put many of the simple rights and services to which they were entitled beyond the means of the poorer people (Matt. 28.12; Luke 3.14; Acts 22.28; 24.26). Landowners wrung extortionate rents from peasant farmers, and townsmen demanded impossibly high dowries from the parents of any girl they proposed to marry. Many families were compelled to sell themselves into slavery as compensation for debts they could not pay, or chose to do so to escape starvation. Prostitution was rife, widows, orphans and homeless folk presented a limitless field for almsgiving, and there were hosts of beggars, often displaying physical disabilities to incite the charity of passers-by.

Then, as now, the well-to-do were apt to assume that most poverty was the fruit of moral turpitude – a view that was positively encouraged by the doctrine that God normally rewarded the righteous with material blessings. So, on top of their destitution, the poor had to bear the added burden of social ambiguity, if not actual ostracism. New Testament historians disagree over this, but the evidence seems to point pretty clearly to the fact that at least the stricter fellowship-groups of *Chaberim*, however generous their charity, kept themselves separate from the *'amme ha-arets* as the Brahmins do from the untouchables in India. The Gospel of John represents the chief priests as saying, 'This crowd who do not know the Law are accursed' (John 7.49), and this accords with the judgment ascribed to the great sage, Hillel: 'No boor is a sinfearer, nor is the *'am ha-arets* pious'.[1]

Several factors contributed to the suspicion that certain types of contact with the common people would contaminate the priestly purity which the more scrupulous of the *Chaberim* sought to maintain. Ever since their partial return from the Babylonian exile, Jews had felt the need to keep their identity distinct from the racially mixed 'peoples of the land'; and even after the latter had adopted Judaism and become separate from the Samaritans, their influence was feared because their customs differed in certain matters of ritual purification. Galilee had been Judaized for only a century before Christ, and although they showed a passionate devotion to the faith, Galileans remained under the old stigma. Quite apart from the suspicion on those grounds, the poorer folk, however pure their Jewish antecedents might be, were in no position to put aside all the tithes, observe all the hours of prayer, carry out all the purifications and obey the details of sabbath-keeping which the Pharisees had prescribed as the right way to fulfil the demands of the Torah. Moreover, many of them could not avoid engaging in forms of employment which the strict jurists considered as ritually, and sometimes morally, contaminating.[2] The more liberal Pharisees sympathized with these difficulties and did not condemn the imperfect obedience. It was imperfect, nonetheless, and in the pursuit of their own perfection they were bound to follow the rules of avoidance. And, to top their burden of inferiority, the common people laboured under the aspersion of ignorance. They were the boors whose lack of education was often contrasted with the enlightenment of the *Chakamim* sages. Aramaic speakers, who probably picked up enough Greek to cope with their cosmopolitan contacts, their lack of Hebrew excluded them from the full liturgy of the synagogue and the subtle expositions of the Scribes, unless they had persevered beyond common expectation under rabbinic instruction. This does not amount to saying that they were thereby excluded from salvation; it merely underlined their personal devaluation, which, in effect, comes to the same thing.

Theologians and politicians may dispute in their own terms about the true meaning of the Kingdom of God, and the time and the manner of its arrival. But the people who best understand it are the poor and the oppressed, because for them it is the object of desperate need and longing, a matter, almost literally, of life or death, though they have few words with which to name it. The vision of God's rule is distilled out of human suffering and frustrated longing. And the *'amme ha-arets* could tell what justice was without benefit of jurists. They had the incomparable imagery of their own scriptures as vocabulary for their hopes: liberation from Egypt, food in the wilderness, a land flowing with milk and honey, the righteous Kingdom of David, the peace of the holy city and the house of prayer for all nations. These visions were confused and imprecise, but unforgettable and poignantly apt. Some massive 'return' was promised, like the home-coming after exile, when God would come back to his forsaken people and they would come back to a state of primal blessedness. There would be a remission of all debts, as in the law of the jubilee, when every unfulfilled obligation that hung over a man, both towards God and his fellows, would be cancelled. And there would be no more hunger; for linked with that law of jubilee in the Torah itself was the promise, not merely of natural plenty but of miraculous fertility (Lev. 25.19–22; 26.3–6). The prophets endorsed this basic hope of hunger appeased and security ensured in very physical images, like those of the Negro Spirituals two thousand years later. 'A time is coming, says the Lord, when the ploughman shall follow hard on the reaper, and he who treads the grapes after him who sows the seed.' 'Nation shall not lift sword against nation, nor ever again be trained for war, and each man shall dwell under his own vine, under his own fig-tree, undisturbed.' 'On this mountain the Lord of Hosts will prepare a banquet of rich fare for all the peoples, a banquet of wines well matured and richest fare' (Amos 9.13; Micah 4.3,4; Isa. 25.6).

The really poor and hungry are prone to regard even the bread that perishes as bread from heaven, and there is little evidence in the Synoptic Gospels that Jesus condemned this naïve lack of discrimination. The prayer, 'Your Kingdom come', is age-long and universal. It rises from blaspheming lips no less than from the pious. From the blood of Abel crying from the ground to Isaiah's protesting 'O Lord, how long?', from the fierce predictions of Magnificat to the dream of Martin Luther King, the oppressed of the earth have called and called for the long delayed restoration of God's just and peaceful reign. We may hesitate to interpret the gospel in such overt terms of political analysis as some liberation theologians are doing, but we cannot deny that the destitute and victimized, 'the little ones', as Jesus called them, were in the forefront of his mind when he went about proclaiming that the Kingdom of God was close at hand. There can be little doubt that the Gospel of Luke is reflecting an authentic element in the thought and teaching of Jesus when it puts into his mouth the words from the scripture: 'The Spirit of Yahweh is upon me, because he has anointed me and sent me to announce good news to the poor, to proclaim release for prisoners and recovery of sight for the blind; to let the broken victims go free, to proclaim the year of Yahweh's favour,' – that is, the year of jubilee (Luke 4.18,19; Isa. 61.1,2; cf. Lev. 25.10). Jesus had taken the plight of the desperate into his understanding of the Kingdom of God. Whatever he meant by God's reign, the announcement of its approach was good news for them and they were the ones who heard him gladly. The corollary must be taken for granted: there were some for whom it was bad news. In the passage quoted from Isaiah the year of the Lord's favour was also the day of God's vengeance.

The phrase, 'parables of the Kingdom', which is not biblical, can be misleading if we suppose that it refers only to those that mention the Kingdom of God directly or by similitude. The advent of God's rule was the constant theme of Jesus' message, and very specific reasons must be found for saying that any of his parables is *not* a parable of the Kingdom. The Gospel of Luke, at the beginning of chapter 18, presents two in succession which are entirely germane to what has just been said.

'And he told them a parable, to the effect that they ought to keep on praying and not lose heart.' So the Evangelist introduces the first parable. But the story itself suggests something far more specific and urgent than that rather generalized religious truism. Consider the two characters in the incident Jesus chose to narrate. 'There was a widow in the city.' Throughout the Bible the widows and the orphans are the representatives of the socially weak. Without a husband to protect her and with few civil rights, the helplessness of a widow was often shamelessly exploited. Jesus knew all about the powerful who 'devour widows' houses'. So this is not simply a story about perseverance in prayer; it speaks of the cry of the poor and helpless. It is about their prayer for the Kingdom.

This widow comes to a judge, asking him to help her to get justice against her adversary. According to the Jewish law of that time, the only case that one judge on his own was allowed to decide was a money matter – 'a debt, a pledge or a portion of an inheritance that is being withheld'.[3] It is clear from the story that the woman had no reason to doubt the strength of her case, if only she could get a hearing. She 'kept coming' to him (v.3); her problem was simply that he would not set a date for the trial. There were many pretexts on which a man could postpone a case with which he did not want to be bothered.

The judge in this incident was representative of all unscrupulous oppression. A judge was required to pass judgment always in the name of God, and with an especial responsibility for widows and orphans (II Chron. 19.5–7; Isa. 10.1–3; Ezek. 22.7), yet this man was godless, and had no respect for humanity. Though the woman kept on coming, he simply ignored her plea. In that impasse Jesus epitomized the entire nature of oppression and impotence.

In the end her persistence wore him down. 'I will vindicate her lest she shatters me with her perpetual coming.' The Greek word reflects Jesus' frequent delight in comical overstatement; it means, literally, 'she will smash my face'. At that point Jesus moves the listeners away from the story to its meaning. If even so unrighteous a judge gives in to a woman's persistence, how much more will God execute justice for those who cry incessantly to him? The next phrase is a bit ambiguous: *'kai makrothumōn ep'autois'*. *Makrothumein* means to withhold anger or punishment for a long time; it often conveys the idea of patient forebearance, so this phrase has been translated in the Revised Version, for example, as 'and he is longsuffering over them'. But this destroys the contrast with the judge's delay, which is the point of the story, and runs counter to the conclusion at the beginning of v.8. Surely the Revised Standard Version is right to turn it into an additional question: 'And will he delay long over them?' It might be rendered even more trenchantly, to bring out the sense of punishment withheld, 'Will he too put off passing judgment in their favour?' Then comes the good news of the Kingdom: 'I tell you, God will execute justice for them *en tachei* – soon, without delay.' That is the word they want to hear. The promise to the

45

oppressed is not 'pie in the sky when you die', nor is Jesus asking them to wait more patiently for a deliverance indefinitely postponed. God will not keep them waiting. In the Acts of the Apostles, the angel who appears to rescue Peter from his prison cell says, 'Get up quickly, *en tachei.*' The Book of Revelation ends with the promise of the exalted Lord, 'Surely I come quickly, *en tachei.*' So this parable ends with the same urgent phrase. The longed-for liberation is imminent. God is very shortly going to keep his promise.

But when he does, will any of those who prayed for it actually respond? When the Kingdom is made manifest, will they enter and live its life? When the Son of Man comes, will he find faith on earth? Whether this is indeed an authentic saying of Jesus, added as an aside, or a comment inserted by the Evangelist, it is a question that the gospel of the Kingdom poses for all who hear it. The next chapter will face it quite specifically.

Meanwhile we have our own pressing question to put to Jesus in response to the parable. How soon is 'quickly'? How near is 'at hand'? That query is one which the Evangelist has already anticipated so precisely twenty-five verses earlier as to lead us to suspect that the whole passage from Luke 17.20 to 18.14 has been compiled as a consecutive discourse, introduced by this very question: 'The Pharisees asked him, "When will the Kingdom of God come?"' The text justifies this view of the Evangelist's intention, for although parts of the section between verses 22 and 37 are paralleled in the great eschatological prophecies of Mark 13 and Matthew 24, there are too many inconsequential verbal differences for anyone to suppose that this Evangelist was here transcribing from either of the other two or from a common source. He is using versions of the tradition that he has come upon independently, and has woven them into a coherent sequence to present the truth he wants to convey. Christians have been so long accustomed to reading short portions of the Gospels, lifted from one or other of them indiscriminately, that they pay very little attention to the differences between the four Evangelists, certainly not to distinctions between the first three. This piecemeal approach has seemed to have received the ratification of New Testament scholars through their analysis of sources and study of the underlying oral traditions. The effect of this is that readers assume that two versions of the same incident or the same parable are saying the same thing; and if they notice any variations of meaning they instinctively try to conflate and reconcile the inconsistencies, instead of letting each text speak for itself. But truth, even historical truth, is not like that and, if we insist that it must be, we impoverish our grasp of it. Biblical scholars during the past twenty-five years have paid more attention to the finished form of the books as we have them, asking what the 'redactors' who gave them this form were trying to say by doing so.

In the Gospels we have four portraits of the same subject, seen through the eyes of four different artists, each working from his own background and in his distinctive style. Restlessly glancing from one portrait to another, we lose them all in a confusion of images. Unless we stand long enough before each in turn to take in its particular perception, we are bound to miss the 'many-splendoured thing', which is the glory of God in the face of Jesus Christ.

This section of Luke's Gospel, then, should not be read as though it were written by Matthew. That Evangelist clearly preferred to present the Kingdom of God in other-worldly terms. As he saw it, it belonged to an age to come, after God had brought the present world order to an end in a cataclysmic act of judgment. There is no doubt that that was what Jesus himself believed, and, if this is ignored, his message cannot be understood aright. The Gospel of Luke accepts that fact, as this section shows, but adds an unexpected twist which, if it is authentic, must be reckoned as a key insight into the gospel that Jesus proclaimed.

The Pharisees' question, 'When will the Kingdom come?'

was tantamount to asking what sort of Kingdom Jesus was expecting. His immediate answer seems to contradict the idea of an eschatological event that will bring this age to an end. 'The Kingdom of God does not come with observation,' as something to be identified by doom-spotters. It is not a precise event to be heralded by portents which those on the look-out can point to, crying: 'See, there!' It is a present reality, a new situation already here 'in your midst', or a new realization making its impact 'within you' (Luke 17.20,21).[4]

How comes it, then, that this Evangelist follows up his seemingly deliberate corrective to Matthew's eschatological emphasis with a passage that is simply another version of parts of the great eschatological prophecy that Matthew elaborated from Mark? Luke is far too subtle an architect of his narrative to be unaware of this apparent contradiction. Indeed, he appears to underline it by repeating the words 'See here! See there!' with two opposing implications. 'People cannot say "See here, see there," about the Kingdom since it is a present, or interior, reality.' 'Don't run after those who say "See here, see there," since it will be like lightning that fills the entire sky.' There could be no more striking way of saying: 'I know the two views of the Kingdom – this-worldly and other-worldly – are contradictory, but both are true.' Precisely because this Evangelist understands that both are true, he is careful to avoid phrases that pin the meaning exclusively to one interpretation or the other. For example, where the Gospel of Matthew uses the theological term, 'the *parousia*' or 'advent, of the Son of Man,' strongly associated with the Second Coming (Matt. 24.27 and 37), the Gospel of Luke opts for the more ambiguous 'the days of the Son of Man' (Luke 17.24, 26 and 30).

That richly evocative phrase is also set at the opening of this section in chapter 17 and sheds its paradoxical light over the whole of it. 'The days are coming when you will long to

see one of the days of the Son of Man, and will not see it'
(Luke 17.22). The end-crisis to which Jesus is looking
throughout this Gospel is his passion. The protracted
journey-motif which the Evangelist has sustained from
chapter 10, verse 51 onwards points to this. In some way
that is defined only by implication, the act of divine intervention and judgment that must usher in the new age is
associated with the climax of that journey in the destiny of
the Son of Man. In his day that Son of Man will resemble
the lightning that illumines the whole sky, but first he
must suffer and be rejected (vv. 24,25). So at this moment
when he turns to his disciples (v. 22), Jesus is represented
as looking ahead to their loss and confusion, and the
confusion of the young church, in the time following that
crisis. It is natural to deduce that this saying has been
derived from the teaching given by and for Christians who
were actually experiencing that confusion and longing at a
later date; yet it is quite conceivable that Jesus should
himself have looked ahead and visualized the anxieties
that would beset his followers. In what is possibly a similar
saying about the future in parable form (Mark 2.19,20) he
had anticipated their coming distress. The longing to see
one of the days of the Son of Man could mean their
yearning for the return of the Lord in the future consummation of God's victory, or it could mean their wistful
memories of the days when he had been with them in the
flesh. Such a backward look is untypical of post-resurrec-
tion thought, and sounds more like our latter-day romanti-
cism. Nonetheless, we should not dismiss the fact that the
church's eschatological hopes are bound to be set upon the
fulfilment of a relationship previously partly known and a
newness already tasted. Continuity with the original experience in Palestine was not only the *raison d'être* of the
Gospels, but also the prospectus of the age to come.
Messiahs of any other temper will not do: 'Don't go off in
pursuit.'

If it is true that this Evangelist holds together, in some kind of tension that we have not yet examined, the eschatological and the here-and-now interpretation of the Kingdom of God, the remainder of chapter 17 certainly exemplifies this. It can be read as a warning of a final divine intervention to wind up this world's history, to overcome and judge its evil, and to bring in a new dispensation of perfect righteousness and fulfilment. 'As it was in the days of Noah, so it will be in the days of the Son of Man. They ate, they drank, they married and were given in marriage until the day when Noah entered the ark and the flood came and destroyed them all.' Another image of unreadiness and doom, and of a means of salvation grasped by a few, is added in the example of Sodom, with a few apt touches: 'they bought, they sold, they planted, they built' – a picture of a more developed civilization. 'So will it be when the Son of Man is unveiled' – the ultimate apocalypse. Then it will be pointless to think of moving to a safer place. There will be no time to change anything, for there will literally be no more time. 'On that day let him who is on the housetop, and his belongings in the house, not come down to carry them away; let him also who is in the fields, or the countryside, not turn back. Remember Lot's wife.' It is a chilling portrayal of catastrophe such as some have experienced in our own century. Here Luke adds familiar words in a new context that gives them an extra bite: 'Whoever seeks to save his life will lose it, but whoever loses it will keep it alive.' So it will be a moment of ultimate segregation, one taken and the other left; however close, however similar they seemed to be, a moment of truth for each one.

But the same passage can be read as a description of the purely historical situation as Jesus saw it. The threatened catastrophe sounds very like the 'final solution' undertaken by a Roman commander whose patience has run out, as many had feared it would. Jesus seems to have believed that his message of the near approach of God's rule and God's way, and his own response to it, presented his nation with an opportunity of deliverance and new life. So he was going to bring the issue to a head. But if other policies prevailed they would prove disastrous. 'If you had known in this your day the things that belong to your peace. But now they are hidden from your eyes' (Luke 19.42). Some are responding to God's nearness, most are indifferent or hostile, on this day when the Son of Man is revealed. Now that the Kingdom of God's nearness has come upon them there is no time to change or delay. If the call comes to you on the rooftop or in the open countryside or, for that matter, while you are mending your nets or keeping your books in the toll-house, you either rise and follow, or you prevaricate, and the moment of decision passes you by. No one who looks back, like Lot's wife, is well placed for the Kingdom of God. So one is taken on the tide of the new way, and the other is left. The Kingdom is good news for some, and bad news for others: good news for the widow, for the poor, for the broken victims who have faith enough; bad news for the unrighteous judge and his kind. Who is ready to welcome the Kingdom? Who is alive to its arrival? Well, you can tell where the dead ones are by the huddle of vultures around them.

So we are back at the two parables: the widow and the judge, the tax-gatherer and the Pharisee – one taken and the other left behind. Both are typical of the ways in which Jesus liked to use stories. They are not allegories; nothing is a symbol of something else. They are realistic anecdotes which make their own point, the first by means of contrast – How different God is! – the second by winning the sympathy of an audience for an unexpected moral judgment. The tax-gatherer, like the widow, belongs to the *'amme ha-arets* and is a victim of disregard. But, whereas the widow's cause was just, the tax-gatherer was patently in the wrong by common estimation. *Morally* he stood condemned for plying a trade in which he could make a living only by extorting more than the required taxes; *ritually* he was defiled by going into the service of Gentiles. On the other hand, while the judge in the first story was godless, the Pharisee in the second would have appealed to those who heard it as the ideal of a pious Jew. Nothing in the story betrays any intention on the part of Jesus to represent the Pharisee as hypocritical or proud, and the force of the parable is diminished if it is read in that sense.[5] The man gratefully acknowledges that it is by God's grace that he has been enabled to live a life so different from that of the poor wretch he can see standing far off across the court of the Israelites at the same hour of prayer. The audience would have considered that man's demeanour, not daring to raise his eyes and beating his breast, as also entirely proper. The comparative valuation of the two characters raised no eyebrows.

Then the tax-gatherer prays, still quite appropriately, 'God be merciful to me a sinner', and at once the audience is trapped by its own orthodoxy and, what is more, by its own experience. For central to its Jewish faith is the belief in Yahweh's *chesed*, his steadfast mercy. If God has answered that cry for mercy at some time or other in their own case, must he not do the same for this abject man? In that case, where does he now stand in God's eyes in comparison with the righteous Pharisee?

Conventional religion had its answers to that disturbing thought. The tax-gatherer, though now within the mercy of God in principle, was still many degrees below the good man. For the genuineness of his repentance must first be proved by penance, restitution and stability in the new life. He was still a long way off in comparison.

That casuistry has never totally convinced anyone, and it must have been to uneasy minds that Jesus delivered the punch line: 'I tell you, this one went down to his house as a righteous man, not the other.' The goodness of the good person is true goodness; but when it is set beside God's immediate acceptance of the one who turns back in supplication, it is seen to be of a different quality, or rather, the relationship with God has a different quality. Those who, for the love of God, set out to achieve a standard of holiness are bound to see themselves and others in relation to that standard, and to a scale of progress, a journey that takes time. Those who know they stand condemned by that standard, and appeal to a mercy that transcends it, see themselves and others in relation only to that mercy. Having come home to God, there is nowhere further for them to travel to. Without probation or delay, they have entered the insouciance and equality of the Kingdom *en tachei*. In the realm of pastoral theology no less than that of eschatological doctrine, the crucial question is, How soon is quickly?

FOUR

Tomorrow Now

1 *He was praying in a certain place, and when he ceased, one of his disciples said to him, 'Lord, teach us to pray as John taught his disciples.'* [2]*And he said to them, 'When you pray, say:*

'Father, hallowed be thy name. Thy kingdom come. [3]*Give us each day our daily bread;* [4]*and forgive us our sins, for we ourselves forgive every one who is indebted to us; and lead us not into temptation.'*

5 *And he said to them, 'Which of you who has a friend will go to him at midnight and say to him, "Friend, lend me three loaves;* [6]*for a friend of mine has arrived on a journey, and I have nothing to set before him";* [7]*and he will answer from within, "Do not bother me; the door is now shut, and my children are with me in bed; I cannot get up and give you anything'?* [8]*I tell you, though he will not get up and give him anything because he is his friend, yet because of his importunity (shamelessness) he will rise and give him whatever he needs.* [9]*And I tell you, Ask, and it will be given you; seek, and you will find; knock, and it will be opened to you.* [10]*For every one who asks receives, and he who seeks finds, and to him who knocks it will be opened.*

14 *Now he was casting out a demon that was dumb; when the demon had gone out, the dumb man spoke, and the people marvelled.* [15]*But some of them said, 'He casts out demons by Be-el'zebul, the prince of demons';* [16]*while others, to test him, sought from him a sign from heaven.* [17]*But he, knowing their thoughts, said to them, 'Every kingdom divided against itself is laid waste, and house falls upon house.* [18]*And if Satan also is divided against himself, how will his kingdom stand? For you say that I cast out demons by Be-el'zebul.* [19]*And if I cast out demons by Be-el'zebul, by whom do your sons cast them out? Therefore they shall be your judges.* [20]*But if it is by the finger of God that I cast out demons, then the kingdom of God has come upon you.* [21]*When a strong man, fully armed, guards his own place,*

his goods are in peace; [22]*but when one stronger than he assails him and overcomes him, he takes away his armour in which he trusted, and divides his spoil.*

For a long time a great deal has been made of the contradiction between what appear to be two distinct notions of the Kingdom of God in the Synoptic Gospels – that which locates it beyond history, when God has terminated the natural order, eradicated all evil in a final judgment, and established his perfect rule over a new heaven and earth, and that which sees the Kingdom as a moral and spiritual transformation, inaugurated by the coming of Jesus, growing and spreading through the response of people to his person and his message. Yet it is now clear that neither of these models would have been recognized by Jesus and his contemporaries as an adequate summary of their expectations. For one thing these alternative stereotypes of the Kingdom both omit the restoration of Israel to a state fulfilling all the prophecies, yet that was central to Jewish hopes for this world and for the world to come. Furthermore, such polarizing of the eschatological and the historical views of the Kingdom of God is an oversimplification, in as much as it ignores the wide variety of speculations about the future that were current.

It was never merely a choice between two views. The spectrum of hopes ranged from the Jewish philosopher Philo's expectation of a national conversion and renewal,[1] through prospects of an earthly Utopia under God, but with no Messiah,[2] or dreams of a human warrior Messiah, reigning over a restored Davidic kingdom in a new golden age,[3] perhaps of limited duration as precursor to the End of the World,[4] to predictions of a transcendent Messiah associated with God in the final cosmic intervention that would usher in the world to come.[5] Amid such a diversity of expectations it is an anachronism to suppose that Jesus was so committed to one definitive theory of the future that he could not have used any other frame of reference.

The Gospel of Luke patently insists that, while there is a tension between the distinct views, they are not mutually exclusive. The Gospel of Matthew prefers, where possible, to identify the coming Kingdom with 'the culmination of the aeon' – or, as we might say, 'the end of time'; yet it includes the parables of the Mustard Seed and the Leaven in the Meal, both pointing to mighty growth from insignificant, hidden beginnings. Even in the so-called 'apocalypse' of Mark 13, which Matthew copies and Luke adapts, the historical crisis of Jerusalem's tragedy is mingled inextricably with the cosmic cataclysm of the end of time, as though there were some mysterious nexus linking earthly event with eternal fulfilment which only the prophets have perceived.

Believing Jews throughout their history, including Jesus of Nazareth, would have said that there certainly is such a connection, and the common factor in both temporal event and ultimate intervention is none other than the hand of God. The same sovereign control that gave, and gives, being and space and time to the cosmos, and may bring space and time to an end, is continuously acting upon the creation, under all the restraints raised by its freedom and contingency, by way of what might be called both intrinsic and voluntary co-operation from within the creation itself. 'Intrinsic co-operation' refers to nature's inexorable movement to bring forth richer, more complex and responsive forms of being and to redress the balance of life by ensuring that, in the long term, every excess of power bears the seeds of its own destruction. 'Voluntary co-operation' means that unique capacity of human beings to open themselves towards God and become fellow-workers with him. By one means or the other, either as life-force and nemesis, or as Father of his children, God is involved in the process and controls the outcome. 'The Lord reigns.' God the Creator was for all time the sole ruler of the universe, though he had chosen for his own purposes to allow the ignorance and rebellion of humanity to run their course. The enterprise, by its own terms, entailed immeasurable frustration, waste and suffering. But in the promised Day of Yahweh, he was going to assert the sovereignty that was always his alone. The change that all Jews were looking for, in one form of expectation or another, was to be a change in the degree of control that God would exercise over their affairs. What was coming was not some abstract state of affairs called the Kingdom; what was coming was God. Their sense of his transcendent greatness was so vivid that such an arrival must imply the end of all that had gone before and a radically new beginning.

That, undeniably, was how Jesus envisaged the coming realization of God's reign. The main brunt of this belief, however, did not lie in excited expectation of 'the end of the world' – a concept that, in any case, suggests to contemporary minds an anything-but-divine climax. It lay in the confidence that God himself was about to take the initiative in a new way in the history of his people and his world. That may still seem an impossible hope to most people in these days, but it is at least one with which they can identify. It rules out the concept of a man-made Kingdom of God. Since God's reign, in the teaching of Jesus, is an eschatological hope, the Kingdom is not something Christians have to 'extend', but something they have to announce. They are not asked to be the Kingdom, but to receive it. They are no more called to build the Kingdom than the wedding guests were invited to prepare the feast. They need to watch their language, especially in the hymns they choose to sing.

But neither is the Kingdom of God to be identified with the heaven of their Christian prayers. Jesus was at one with the Pharisees in believing in life after death, in a redress of this world's injustice in some paradise or 'Abraham's

57

bosom', and in a final resurrection and resurrection life. But that is not what he meant by God's reign. He looked for something much nearer to the age-long dream of the oppressed, much nearer to the visions of the great prophets of his race. He believed as they had done that this world was not to be written off, still less was it to be the scene of God's failure. Kingdom Come was synonymous with 'Your will be done on earth as in heaven.' There was to be a restoration of Israel. raised to life out of her own ruins, as prophets had said. The little people, the little flock, were to stop being afraid, because it was their Father's good pleasure to give his Kingdom to them, that is, to give them the experience of his full sovereignty, his justice and mercy and loving control over the life of this earth.

Readers of the New Testament think too readily about the Kingdom as though it were a realm or a regime distinguishable from the one who rules over it. British people can speak of the United Kingdom without having the reigning monarch in mind, but it would have been unthinkable for Jesus to imagine that God's Kingdom had an independent connotation of that kind. When Jesus came back into Galilee and proclaimed that the Kingdom or Reign of God had drawn near, his hearers would have understood him to mean that God was at the gates with deliverance in his hands. His announcement was in effect the perennial invitation of the prophets, '"Come back to me," says the Lord, "and I will come back to you"' – which the Epistle of James translates with the same word of approach as Jesus had used: 'Draw near to God and he will *draw near* to you.' To the poor and overburdened and outcast the words would have promised that the God of rescue was at hand, with a new deal of justice and acceptance, to take full control of the world. The yearning to which the first preaching of Jesus appealed is accurately reflected in the ancient collect, originally written to be addressed to Christ, which is appointed in the Book of Common Prayer for the Sunday before Christmas: 'O Lord, raise up, we pray thee, thy power and come among us, and with great might succour us . . .'

Anyone who heard Mr Alec McCowen's perceptive recitals of the Gospel of Mark in the late 1970s must have been newly astonished by the breathless onrush of incidents that erupted from the moment of Jesus' return to Galilee after his baptism by John. They tumble, one after another, 'immediately', 'straightway'. His preaching in the synagogue at Capernaum astonishes the congregation. He casts out an unclean spirit from a sufferer. He raises Peter's mother-in-law from a fever and cures many with various diseases who gather about the door. As he moves on to other villages even leprosy yields to him and the news spreads. Back in Capernaum he releases the paralysed man, both from sickness and guilt, addresses a crowd by the shore, recruits a tax official and is entertained by him and his like, begins to encounter criticism which turns to angrier conflict when he heals on the sabbath a man with a withered hand. All the time the crowd surrounding him multiplies. What the Gospel is presenting is a picture of the power of God unleashed in direct combat against the long tyranny of evil, and the tragic failure of the most devoted servants of God to recognize what was happening, so that they actually ranged themselves on the wrong side. The gravity of their blindness lay not in their misjudgment of Jesus, which was understandable in view of his seemingly easy-going admission of sinners into his following. Their error was to see the evidence without perceiving that God himself had come directly upon the scene to take control. His Kingdom, his sovereignty, was at hand.

'He was driving out a demon of dumbness, and when the demon had come out the dumb man began to speak' (Luke 11.14). Without venturing upon the vast subject of demonology in the ancient world, a few facts need to be recalled in order to appreciate the force of this passage. Belief in demons evolved from two sources: primitive animistic belief in powerful intelligences embodied in trees, springs or wild beasts, especially of the desert (that is the significance of saying that Jesus was 'with the wild beasts' during his temptation in the wilderness); and the Jewish attitude to the gods of other nations which, as they became fully monotheist themselves, they relegated to a subordinate order of hostile beings, sometimes associated with the moon and stars. Matthew's Gospel, for example, speaks of the epileptic boy who was brought to Jesus after the Transfiguration as 'moon-struck' or 'taken by Selene' – a notion that lives on in our word 'lunatic'. These destructive powers were thought to be under the command of Satan, and were specially active in the hours of darkness. At the sound of the cockcrow their power faded and they dispersed. That is what lies behind the warning given to Simon Peter: 'Satan has desired to have you all, and *before* cockcrow you will deny me thrice.'

Demons were commonly categorized in groups of seven. There were, for example, those that attacked the natural powers of sight, hearing, smell, speech, taste, procreation and life. This may have contributed to much later Christian teaching about the seven deadly sins (Luke 11.26). Professional exorcists were common enough, and their most frequent method of mastering the demons was a recitation of the names of the great angels who opposed them in the power of God. This belief in the magical potency of a name is demonstrated in the story in the Acts of the Apostles of the exorcists at Ephesus who tried to use the name of Jesus in this way (Acts 19.13). On the same principle, if the exorcist could get hold of the name of the demon, he would repeat it, cutting off a syllable each time, and thus reducing the demon to an impotent nonentity. So, in dealing with Shabriri, the spirit of blindness, an exorcist would say to the afflicted person, 'Arm thyself against Shabriri, beriri, riri, iri, ri.' But all believed that, behind the incantations, stood the power of God who alone was able ultimately to quell the forces of evil. The war between angelic and demonic powers was to continue, however, only until the great day of the consummation of the age, when God would pass judgment on every manifestation of evil and resume his total sovereignty. That was the reign of God to which all were looking forward, though they disagreed as to the way in which it would come, and this expectation set a term to the partial ascendancy of evil. So, according to Matthew's Gospel, the demoniacs of Gadara cried out against Jesus, 'Have you come here to torment us *before* our time?'

Those who have experienced the life of animistic societies in our own day find much of this strangely familiar and know that within the living context of such a world view, it 'works' with remarkable success in cases that Western medicine would call psychopathic or psychosomatic. Any attempt to adopt in practice a cosmology that is essentially exotic and remote from one's own is liable to induce quite serious mental disturbance and should be avoided. But it is not difficult to imagine the reactions to Jesus' healing powers of those to whom such ideas were commonplace.

While the Galilean crowd marvelled at Jesus' successful exorcisms, there were some who could not accept the obvious implications. For in their eyes Jesus' teaching and manner of life was too contrary to their idea of piety for him to qualify as an agent of any divine power. His control of demons must therefore be gained by using the name of their own ruler, Beelzebul or Satan. Jesus counters this on two scores. Can Satan work against himself? And what about other Jewish exorcists? The true interpretation is just the opposite of theirs: 'If it is by the finger of God that I am casting out demons, then be sure God's sovereignty has overtaken you.' That retort takes the issue far beyond the point of their accusation. They had insinuated that Jesus was not in the same class as the true exorcists who invoked angelic powers. But now he is claiming that he is indeed different from the other Jewish exorcists; something new and unparalleled is taking place. The cures wrought by those others had not been seen as evidence that the great day of God's rule was dawning. Where was the difference? Simply in this, that Jesus conjured no angels, recited no incantations. In his own personality the power of God confronted the kingdom of moral and physical anarchy. He charged the demons on his own authority to relinquish their power. It was in the same spirit, according to other evangelists, that he met the massed powers of evil in the night of Gethsemane. 'The ruler of this world is coming, and has no hold over me.' 'Do you think I could not appeal to my Father, and he would send more than twelve legions of angels?' Without intermediary or supernatural aid, the finger and the Spirit of God was active in him. What is more, according to all three Synoptists, he had actually given that authority to the Twelve. The vivid analogy of the strong man overwhelmed by a stronger is told in the terms of single combat. *He* takes from *him* the panoply in which he trusted. The victor might be Jesus, or even a disciple, but the implication of the parable is that fundamentally it is the Lord God himself who has come directly upon the scene as victor and king. And that can only mean that the Day of the Lord, the End Time, the culmination of history, is at hand.

'At hand' – how near is that? The phrase does not occur in this passage in Luke 11, but it is part of the original proclamation of Jesus according to Mark's Gospel ('The time is fulfilled and the Kingship of God is at hand') and, according to Matthew, part of the Baptist's message too. The verb in Greek is formed from a word that means 'near'. It signifies a coming close, an approach, but it has not quite the same sense as to arrive. So, at the end of the agony in Gethsemane, Jesus says to the sleeping apostles, 'Wake up, let's go. The betrayer *has approached*,' and in the next verse we read, 'And immediately, while he was still speaking, Judas *arrived*.' It is the first of these two verbs that Jesus applied to the Kingdom of God. That subtle distinction between nearness and arrival is what separates the future from the present. God's rule is still in the future but, as Jesus understood it, only just.

What gave him that absolute assurance that the Kingdom of God, the ultimate sovereignty of God at the end of time, was so close at hand? Others should have deduced it from the 'signs' of God's final victorious challenge to the powers of disease and possession, sin and estrangement. But the conviction of Jesus was prior to those demonstrations. His certainty that God was at the very gates was the *source* from which he derived his authority as teacher and healer. How did he become so convinced? Facile explorations into the spiritual perceptions of Jesus are an arrogant intrusion. But the plain evidence of the Gospels themselves points consistently to one thing as the hidden germ from which his overwhelming conviction sprang. Jesus knew the absolute nearness of God existentially. From the nearness of God to himself came the certainty that God's Kingdom, God's very self in sovereignty, had come within range. This intimate linking of the personal spirituality of Jesus to his insistence that the consummation of the age was near explains the equal emphasis which the Synoptic Gospels lay upon the Kingship of God and the Fatherhood of God, and the personal slant that Jesus gave to both of these.

The interaction between personal relationship to God and public announcement of the Kingdom finds its perfect expression, of course, in the Lord's Prayer. 'And he was praying in a certain place, and when he ceased, one of his disciples said to him, "Lord, teach us to pray, as John taught his disciples." And he said to them, "When you pray, say: Father, hallowed be your name."'

No teacher of prayer can do other than pass on what he himself has learnt. John the Baptist must have taught his disciples to pray as he did. The Lord's Prayer must be an epitome of the way Jesus himself prayed: *his* prayer. Not in so many words, perhaps; the recitation of set words seems to have been contrary to his spirituality. But these bare, terse phrases, which Luke's version emphasizes, sum up the entire burden of Jesus' vivid relationship to God. And he gave to those who were close to him the right and the invitation to pray as he had learnt to pray. 'When you pray say, "Father".' The one word – Abba in the Aramaic – is probably the true original version – not 'Our Father', nor 'Father in the heavens', but simply, 'Abba'. Mark's account of the prayer in Gethsemane makes a point of saying that Jesus used that word, crying, 'Abba, Father, if it be possible let this cup pass from me.' In that account, 'Abba' is a pointless addition unless the actual word carried a special significance far beyond the general idea of the Fatherhood of God. Why, again, should Paul say twice over that the Spirit of God enables Christians to use that word when they pray, unless it indicated a relationship with God of an unusual intimacy? Joachim Jeremias and other scholars, though not all, have been convinced by the textual evidence that no other Jewish prayer of the same period ever *addressed* God directly as 'Abba', but that this form was used by Jesus in every one of his recorded prayers, except the cry from the Cross. If that is the case, it means that it was a well-known idiosyncrasy of Jesus to use, when speaking to God, this homely word by which a Jewish child addressed his father, and his preference for that word, Abba, expressed a relationship of extraordinary directness and intensity.

The accounts of the baptism of Jesus in all three Synoptics suggest that it was for him a decisive experience, confirming in him through the Holy Spirit his inner consciousness that he stood in relation to God as a son to a father. Such direct access must have come as a revelation, though some charismatic teachers of that time claimed something of the same familiarity with God. To the Pharisees God's nearness was to be found in the Torah; to the priestly Sadducees God's nearness was to be found in the sacrifices that preserved his covenant with Israel. But this unmediated knowledge of God as a child knows a parent was an unprecedented nearness. It sent Jesus first to the wilderness to wrestle with its implications, and then back to Galilee to announce those implications: 'The final breakthrough of God's sovereignty is at hand; turn to meet it.' Now, as he began to talk about God and his coming rule, this man did not refer to the scriptures or quote the rabbis. He spoke with the unassuming certainty of someone with immediate access to ultimate truth. His knowledge of the Father did not contradict the traditional teaching, yet it was independent of it, and could go beyond it without a moment's hesitation. 'It was said in the past, but I say . . .'

Yet Jesus does not seem to have regarded his closeness to God as his own unique possession. Though his ambiguous assumption of the title 'Son of Man' shows that he came to accept a special role in relation to the approaching Kingdom, he clearly believed that the nearness of God that was his must be open for all. He taught his followers to say 'Father' and to be as importunate and as uninhibited as children. In the most strikingly personal saying in the Synoptic Gospels, he seems to betray a sense of isolation. 'No one knows a son so well as his own father does, and no one knows a father as his son does, or any others to whom the son has made him known' (Matt. 11.27; Luke 10.22). To make God known as he knew him clearly became the overmastering desire of Jesus. That is the meaning of his prayer, 'Hallowed be your name' – Holy, holy, holy is your name and your name is Abba. You have hidden it from the learned and wise and revealed it to infants who use it naturally.

Scholars have pointed out the resemblance between the opening petitions of the Lord's Prayer and of the ancient Aramaic prayer called the Kaddish which ended the synagogue services in Jesus' day. It begins: 'Exalted and hallowed be his great name in the world which he created according to his will. May he let his kingdom rule . . .' The hallowing of the divine name is a frequent theme in the Old Testament. It means responding to what God is, his holiness, by being like him as a community, a holy people, and so revealing his true nature to other peoples by means of this likeness. Leviticus contains the call, 'You shall therefore be holy for I am holy' (Lev. 11.45), and in the previous chapter it runs: 'I will show myself holy among those that are near me, and before *all* the people I will be glorified' (Lev. 10.3). The well-known promise in Ezekiel, 'I will give you a new heart and put a new spirit within you,' is preceded by the words, 'I will hallow my great name which has been profaned among those nations. When they see that I reveal my holiness through you, the nations will know that I am the Lord' (Ezek. 36.23). So the prayer, 'Father, hallowed be your name,' which is echoed in the Fourth Gospel as 'Father, glorify your name', which Jesus prayed when the Greeks came seeking him, might be paraphrased as: 'Let us to whom you have come so near that we know your true nature as Abba, now reflect that nature so that others may see it in what we do and are.' It is a return to the old covenant ideal of the imitation of God (see pp.19f.).

Jesus prayed this prayer and named the childlike name, not in his teaching only but in his deliberate imitation of God's nature in the way he treated people. Since God had come so close and was now so accessible, Jesus too made himself available to all. Because God loved unconditionally, Jesus accepted people without checking their credentials, so that the most substantial criticism that could be levelled against him was that he seemed to treat sin too lightly, the very opposite to holiness. It has been well said of Jesus: 'Proclaiming that his God was now at work, he made him visible and tangible. People heard God preached and saw him in action.'[6] The Gospels portray Jesus as enacting, and calling others to start enacting, God's way of dealing with people in the light of the nearness of God which had come upon them. 'Be merciful as your Father is merciful.' 'Pray for your persecutors, so shall you be children of your heavenly Father who makes his sun rise on good and bad alike and sends the rain on honest and dishonest.' 'Be perfect as your Father is perfect.' This joyful ideal is exactly encapsulated in what may originally have been more of a parable than a theological statement in the Gospel of John; in fact Professor C. H. Dodd called it the parable of the apprenticed son: 'The son can do nothing on his own; he does only what he sees his father doing. What the father does, the son does.' (John 5.19). So 'Hallowed be your name' is the same prayer, in effect, as 'Your Kingdom, your sovereignty come,' which can in its turn be paraphrased as 'Your will be done on earth as in heaven,' the phrase which the Gospel of Matthew adds.

But just at this point it is vital to remember that it is a prayer for the new age. It is at the door but it has not arrived. It could not have arrived, since its coming must involve the end of this age, the judgment, and the universal sovereignty of the Father. It still belongs to the future, but only just. It has come so near, or rather, God has come so near, that those who have faith may begin to live the life of the Kingdom, may begin to enact the nature of the Father, *in advance of that Kingdom's arrival*. The Kingdom in the teaching of Jesus is always 'not yet', but so close that, like a great star approaching, it is exercising a gravitational pull upon the earth that changes everything. He calls his followers to respond proleptically, *to live the future now*.

That is the hidden thrust of the next phrase in the prayer – one which seems at first sight the simplest of all: 'Give us each day our daily bread'. The only reason for doubting that translation is that both the Gospels that give us the Lord's Prayer, while they differ on many other details, use at this point a previously non-existent word, *epiousion*, which is not one of the natural words for 'daily'. In fact Origen, writing in the second century AD, asserted that *epiousion* did not occur anywhere in Greek literature or in common usage, and had probably been coined by the Evangelists to translate some Aramaic phrase passed down by the disciples themselves. The word has, in fact, turned up in an Egyptian papyrus of the fifth century AD, where it means a ration of food; that may simply show that the word in the Christian prayer had become common parlance by that time. But a century before that papyrus was written, Jerome, who had translated the Bible into Latin, said in his commentary on the Gospel of Matthew that he had seen a copy of an Aramaic 'Gospel of the Hebrews', of which no copies now exist but which was compiled soon after our four Gospels, in which the word *māchar*, 'tomorrow's', was used. The word in our Gospels, *epiousion*, might, with considerable grammatical strain, mean 'for existence' – that is to say, 'the bread we need for life'. But an easier derivation links it with the common phrase, *hē epousa hēmera*, 'the day following', which occurs several times in the Acts of the Apostles; and this gives us the meaning: 'Give us tomorrow's bread today'. 'Tomorrow's food' is the life of the long-awaited Kingdom of God, so often pictured as a banquet, the bread of heaven to which both the pious and the hungry were looking forward. So this phrase in the Lord's Prayer is in line with those that precede it. It is a cry for the presence and the rule of God which belongs to the future, but which Jesus bids his followers boldly to claim as theirs already, day by day. What holy impetuosity! 'From the days of John the Baptist until now the Kingdom of heaven has been subjected to violence and men of violence take it by force' (Matt. 11.12).

That was one way of putting it, to underline the boldness required for the response that Jesus was making to the near approach of God. But the initiative was on God's side. It was *he* who had stolen a march on all human expectations. When Jesus says, 'If I, by the finger of God, am driving out demons, then be sure God's Kingdom has overtaken you,' the word is not the usual 'has come near' but a more striking term, *ephthasen eph' humas*; it means to get there first, to anticipate, and fits very well the idea of living tomorrow now.

So does the parable that follows the Lord's Prayer in the Gospel of Luke, a faintly humorous story, not unlike that of the unrighteous judge. The family man is knocked up by his friend in the middle of the night, a friend who is asking for tomorrow's bread now, at this preposterous hour! 'I tell you,' says Jesus, 'that though he will not give him anything on account of his friendship, yet because of his *effrontery* he will get up and give him whatever he needs.' The word is much stronger than the usual 'importunity'. It means lack of shame, defiance of the proprieties, all the things in Jesus' own behaviour that gave offence to the establishment, the audacity of those who dare to reflect the nature and the rule of God as though it were already triumphant. That is not yet the case; but ask and it will be given, seek and you will find, knock and God's Kingdom will be opened.

God's direct control of affairs, which is what the Kingdom means, is strictly unimaginable. Humanity has dreamed of it and does so still, but the dreams are partial glimpses only. Faith avers that the Kingdom will come in God's good time. It will be his creation and his gift. It is not a heavenly after-life; it is not the church; it is not a political manifesto. It remains a promise and a vision for the life of this world – but not a remote hope. It is near, and its outlines are discernible, because God is near and knowable. The nature and the ways of the Kingdom are God's nature, God's ways.

So the proper response to this good news is two-fold: mystical and revolutionary. It entails cultivating that inti-mate relationship with God as 'Abba' to which Jesus invited people, and acting out in the relationships and situations of this world the nature and the values of that God. Jesus calls those who will follow him into the absurdity of entering, or receiving,[7] the Not-Yet now; and the entering consists of putting that absurdity into practice. 'Not everyone who says to me, "Lord, Lord", shall enter the Kingdom of heaven, but he who does the will of my Father who is in heaven.' In the simplest terms, the way of the Kingdom means knowing the Father and doing what we see the Father doing. There can be no question of postponing the embarrassment of the public doing until one has first perfected the private knowing; that is a dodging of the challenge much favoured by the pious. In reality the two parts of the equation advance concurrently. It is precisely by attempting the outrageous effrontery of acting under God's control in a society that is not yet submitted to it that the faithful make new discoveries about him and learn to know him more truly. And, because such obedience is contrary to the way of the world, this way of the Kingdom needs to be embarked upon in company with other adventurers, learning with one another.

There are, in fact, innumerable examples of 'living the future now'. Two families with young children, overtaken by the social decline of the inner city in which they lived: when the time came when they might have moved out to a more desirable suburb with better schools and facilities, as others were doing, they chose instead to stay behind with those who could not get out, because, as they said, they would not implant in their children's minds an idea of grading people which was not in God's mind. By staying on they were instrumental in encouraging their neighbours to form a housing co-operative which, bit by bit, gave them all responsibility for managing and renovating their own homes. Those two couples were living the future, on which, in the light of their understanding of God, they set their hopes, in anticipation of its arrival; but their former friends, including many of their fellow church members, consider them culpably irresponsible towards their children.

A more widely known example is the settlement named 'The Oasis of Peace' half-way between Jerusalem and Tel Aviv.[8] It consists of an equal number of Arab and Israeli families – Jews, Christians and Muslims, each true to their own culture and religion – who have come together to demonstrate that all can live as neighbours and colleagues in one community. They are learning the painful arts of understanding and reconciliation, and passing them on to thousands of the younger generation through the training courses of their School for Peace. Many of their former associates in the Israeli and Arab communities are highly suspicious and even outraged; but these pioneers believe they are simply living the only acceptable future in advance of its arrival.

Even the simple act of total unconditional forgiveness is an actualizing of the Kingdom that has not yet come. The world's morality is a system of personal rights and claims, merits and deserts, rewards and punishments. Letting off the wrong-doer without repayment, settling without compensation for injury, writing off debts, forgiveness without evidence of repentance, are regarded as dangerously easy-going and even unethical. Many in Jesus' day would have said that the forgiveness of sins, being God's prerogative, belonged to the age to come, the jubilee amnesty, when the victory over evil had been won, and all things finally reconciled. But Jesus taught his disciples to pray: 'Give us today the forgiveness that is promised for the age of the Messiah.' When forgiveness has become virtually impossible its truly eschatological character is revealed. It had reached that degree of impossibility for the senior girls of a school in Uganda when they knew that the fathers or brothers of some of them had murdered the families of others of them in the inter-tribal struggle. Yet, when it seemed that mutual hatred must make the shared life of a boarding school unthinkable, they saw themselves with new eyes as victims together of an evil that was about to take over their whole generation; and they wept, embracing each other as Christians in a superhuman forgiveness. 'As we forgive our debtors' means nothing less than 'We choose

71

to be fool enough, your fools, to live the life of that Kingdom now, in the forgiveness of all who have wronged us.'

FIVE

Eating and Drinking

45 *When the chief priests and the Pharisees heard his parables, they perceived that he was speaking about them.* [46]*But when they tried to arrest him, they feared the multitudes, because they held him to be a prophet.*

1 *And again Jesus spoke to them in parables, saying,* [2]*'The kingdom of heaven may be compared to a king who gave a marriage feast for his son,* [3]*and sent his servants to call those who were invited to the marriage feast; but they would not come.* [4]*Again he sent other servants, saying, "Tell those who are invited, Behold, I have made ready my dinner, my oxen and my fat calves are killed, and everything is ready; come to the marriage feast."* [5]*But they made light of it and went off, one to his farm, another to his business,* [6]*while the rest seized his servants, treated them shamefully, and killed them.* [7]*The king was angry, and he sent his troops and destroyed those murderers and burned their city.* [8]*Then he said to his servants, "The wedding is ready, but those invited were not worthy.* [9]*Go therefore to the thoroughfares, and invite to the marriage feast as many as you find."* [10]*And those servants went out into the streets and gathered all whom they found, both bad and good; so the wedding hall was filled with guests.*

11 *'But when the king came in to look at the guests, he saw there a man who had no wedding garment;* [12]*and he said to him, "Friend, how did you get in here without a wedding garment?" And he was speechless.* [13]*Then the king said to the attendants, "Bind him hand and foot, and cast him into the outer darkness; there men will weep and gnash their teeth."* [14]*For many are called, but few are chosen.'*

Matt. 21.45–22.14

1 *One sabbath when he went to dine at the house of a ruler who*

belonged to the Pharisees, they were watching him. ²And behold, there was a man before him who had dropsy. ³And Jesus spoke to the lawyers and Pharisees, saying, 'Is it lawful to heal on the sabbath, or not?' ⁴But they were silent. Then he took him and healed him, and let him go. ⁵And he said to them, 'Which of you, having an ass or an ox that has fallen into a well, will not immediately pull him out on a sabbath day?' ⁶And they could not reply to this.

7 Now he told a parable to those who were invited, when he marked how they chose the places of honour, saying to them, ⁸'When you are invited by any one to a marriage feast, do not sit down in a place of honour, lest a more eminent man than you be invited by him; ⁹and he who invited you both will come, and say to you, "Give place to this man," and then you will begin with shame to take the lowest place. ¹⁰But when you are invited, go and sit in the lowest place, so that when your host comes he may say to you, "Friend, go up higher"; then you will be honoured in the presence of all who sit at table with you. ¹¹For every one who exalts himself will be humbled, and he who humbles himself will be exalted.'

12 He said also to the man who had invited him, 'When you give a dinner or a banquet, do not invite your friends or your brothers or your kinsmen or rich neighbours, lest they also invite you in return, and you be repaid. ¹³But when you give a feast, invite the poor, the maimed, the lame, the blind, ¹⁴and you will be blessed, because they cannot repay you. You will be repaid at the resurrection of the just.'

15 When one of those who sat at table with him heard this, he said to him, 'Blessed is he who shall eat bread in the kingdom of God!' ¹⁶But he said to him, 'A man once gave a great banquet, and invited many; ¹⁷and at the time for the banquet he sent his servant to say to those who had been invited, "Come; for all is now ready." ¹⁸But they all alike began to make excuses. The first said to him, "I have bought a field, and I must go out and see it; I pray you, have me excused." ¹⁹And another said, "I have bought five yoke of oxen, and I go to examine them; I pray you, have me excused." ²⁰And another said, "I have married a wife, and therefore I cannot come." ²¹So the servant came and reported this to his master. Then the householder in anger said to his servant, "Go out quickly to the streets and lanes of the city, and bring in the poor and maimed and blind and lame." ²²And the servant said, "Sir, what you commanded has been done, and still there is room." ²³And the master said to the servant, "Go out to the highways and hedges, and compel

people to come in, that my house may be filled. ²⁴*For I tell you, none of those men who were invited shall taste my banquet."'*

Luke 14.1–24

The Gospels are almost as full of meals as of miracles. This is not altogether surprising, seeing that they were written for a religious movement that had a sacramental meal as its central act of worship and testimony. It was truly perceptive of the detractors of Jesus to pick on this, if indeed they did, as characteristic of him. 'The Son of Man came eating and drinking, and they say, "Look at him, a glutton and a drinker"' (Matt. 11.19). People could scarcely have failed to notice the contrast between him and the ascetic John the Baptist in this respect. It is clear both from his practice and his teaching that a meal was a highly significant symbol in the mind of Jesus Christ.

It is commonly said in the commentaries that the consummation of God's sovereignty at the end of the age was frequently portrayed as a triumphal banquet in Jewish expectations at the time of Jesus. But in fact the evidence of this is very scarce. Only one passage in the Old Testament uses the image of a feast to depict the eschatological Kingdom. 'On this mountain the Lord of Hosts will prepare a banquet of rich fare for all the peoples, a banquet of wines well matured and richest fare, well-matured wines strained clear. On this mountain the Lord will swallow up that veil that shrouds all the peoples . . . he will swallow up death forever' (Isa. 25.6). In later Jewish literature that section of the Book of Enoch known as the Similitudes, which may have been circulating early enough to influence the language of the New Testament, though many give it a later date, contains a single reference to the Messianic or heavenly banquet in chapter 62 verses 13 and 14: 'The righteous and elect ones shall be saved on that Day, and from thenceforth they shall never see the faces of the sinners and oppressors.

The Lord of the Spirits will abide over them; they shall eat and rest and rise with that Son of Man forever and ever.'[1] References to the age to come as a feast are very infrequent in the other apocryphal books of Hellenistic Judaism and, in any case, were written well after the time of Jesus.[2] So it looks as though the prevalence of this imagery in the Gospels is derived from Jesus' own partiality for it and the significance he gave to it.

What it meant to him as a figure of the Kingdom of God begins to emerge from a comparison of the two versions of one parable in the Gospels of Matthew and Luke. The first of these Evangelists, as has already been said, betrays a leaning towards the fully eschatological emphasis in his presentation of the message of Jesus Christ. It is today a healthy reminder to a church that has, generally speaking, become too prone to settle down as the Sadducee party did to an ecclesial and ethical religion, devoid of supernatural and other-worldly aspirations. It is necessary to remember that Jesus clearly believed that God's rule, when it eventually breaks in upon this world, will be distinctly 'out of this world', a radical ending of history as previously experienced. What further needs to be grasped is that, while he endorsed with total conviction that apocalyptic expectation, in common with the Pharisees and most of the Essenes, Jesus added his peculiar rider, drawn from his experience of intimacy with God, that it was time to start living as though that future were already here. But the Gospel of Matthew, faithful to the primary conviction of Jesus, misses the sheer originality of the nuance he gave to it, and stresses the eschatology pure and simple.

The central figure in its version of the parable is a king who is giving a feast at the marriage of his son (Matt. 22.1–10). It is a clear allegory of God and his Messiah-Son, as the early church perceived the person of Jesus. The servants are sent out according to the courtesies of those days to tell the guests that the time has come and the dinner is ready. The

Evangelist is so eager to get on to the main thrust of his story that he takes for granted the initial invitation; but he enlarges on the opulence of the menu to emphasize that enormity of the guests' rebuff. For they made light of it. It was a matter of no concern to them. Offering no excuses, they went off, as if it were a fresh whim, to the farm or the business, and others beat up the messengers and even killed them. It is a portrayal of extreme hostility to the heralds of the impending new day, and every detail reinforces the outrage of their rejection so as to prepare the way for the king's violent reprisal. At this point (v.7) the allegory of a wedding feast is momentarily forgotten in a realistic report of a punitive expedition and the burning of a city. One begins to suspect that whoever told the story in this form had the inhabitants of Jerusalem in mind. Then, just as suddenly, (v.8) we are brought back to the earlier framework. The servants are told that the original guests were unworthy and others are to be called in to replace them. We are not told that they are poorer or more unfortunate folk, only that they are to be gathered in from the main roads, as though they were travellers passing through, strangers with no house of their own in the place.

The allegory is addressing what was a pressing question for Christians of a Jewish background: why the Gentiles were being called into the kingdom of God in place of the chosen people. That dilemma may have dictated the thrust that this version gives to the story. In the light of other sayings and actions attributed to Jesus in the Gospels it would seem too cavalier to say that this interpretation is altogether foreign to the thought of Jesus. Nevertheless, taking note of his usually preferred style of story-telling it seems fairly clear that this is not how he originally told this story and that something of its authentic force has been lost. As a reminder of the more characteristic way in which Jesus liked to tell a real-life anecdote and leave it to speak for itself, it is revealing to look at what was probably a separate parable which the Gospel of Matthew has tacked on to the other as an appendix in verses 11–13. Dr Eta Linnemann, who wrote with illuminating perception about the parables, suggested that it may have run rather like this before the Evangelist added a few of his own most characteristic phrases:

> The kingdom of heaven is like a king who arranged a wedding for his son. And the wedding hall was filled with guests. But when the king came in to see the guests, he found there a man with no wedding garment on, and he said to him, 'Friend, how did you get in here without a wedding garment on?' But he was speechless. Then the king said to the attendants, 'Take him by his hands and feet and throw him out.'[3]

Custom required, not a special costume appropriate for weddings, but simply that one's clothes be freshly washed. To come in soiled clothes was insulting because it indicated lack of preparation. The story is another short, forceful reminder of the constant message in Jesus' teaching – something is imminent; don't be taken unawares but, instead, start imagining that it is already here. You have been invited to God's banquet. Rate that as your top priority and get ready.

The Gospel of Matthew has tried to answer a different question in the minds of its readers – 'If the Jews have been found unready, can we be sure that Gentiles will prove any more worthy?' The Evangelist prepares the way for his answer by referring to the wayfarers who were 'gathered in', according to the previous parable, as 'both good and bad' (v.10), words borrowed from his version of the parables of the drag-net and of the tares in the wheat (13.30–31, 47–48). So the entry of Gentiles into the church does not guarantee that all of them are truly obedient to the rule of God and vested in the robe of salvation. Guided more by theological purpose than by realism and the likelihood of finding people off the streets who are wearing freshly laundered clothes, he consigns the offending guest to the outer darkness and to weeping and gnashing of teeth – his regular symbols of eternal damnation (8.12; 13.42,50). As has already been said, such allegorical treatment of a story in which the various elements are symbols of something else, is different from Jesus' way of presenting an anecdote, comically exaggerated perhaps, which made its own point just as it stood without elaboration.

The Gospel of Luke sets its version of the parable of the banquet in a carefully constructed framework (Luke 14.1–24), just as it does the parable of the widow and the judge, as was remarked in chapter 3 of this book. But, whereas in that case the Evangelist succeeded in creating a remarkably coherent, if not historically accurate, sequence, here the stringing together of various meal-time episodes produces a patently artificial continuity. In verse 1 he places the incident of the sabbath day healing and the controversial question about rescuing a beast on the sabbath in the home of a Pharisee who had invited Jesus to dine. It is not an impossible setting for such a test, though the synagogue, where Matthew's Gospel places it, is more appropriate. But even if there were such a trap laid for Jesus in a leading Pharisee's home, it is not likely that such a scrupulous man would have given a dinner party for a large crowd of guests on the Sabbath evening, so the next incident, verses 7–11, must have happened in some other circumstance. This ironical observation of guests who arrived at table at different times, as was customary, but were jockeying for the best places, might have been made at any time. As shrewd advice it belongs to the same genre as the charming passage on dinner etiquette in the Book of Ecclesiasticus chapter 32. Whatever its intention, it clearly has no connection with the parable of the discourteous guests which is to follow later.

The next paragraph, verses 12–14, gives a characteristic

example of Jesus' awareness of the 'little ones', the poor and disadvantaged, to which this Gospel draws particular attention. Moreover the mention of the four specific types – 'the poor, the mutilated, the lame, the blind' – is repeated in that order in the parable that follows. Yet, if one were confronted by these three verses on their own, and asked to place them in the most fitting context in the Gospel, one would most naturally attach them to the comparable sayings in Luke 6.32–34, where the same form of argument is used. It would then read:

If you love those who love you, what credit is that to you? Even sinners love those who love them. And if you do good to those from whom you hope to receive, what credit is that to you? Even sinners lend to sinners to receive as much again. And when you give a dinner or a banquet do not invite your friends, for they will invite you in return and you will be repaid. But when you give a feast, invite the poor, the maimed, the lame, the blind and you will find happiness since they cannot repay you.

This somewhat Quixotic treatment of the poor and disadvantaged reads very like an authentic word of Jesus about the life of God's Kingdom, an example of the effrontery of living the future now; but its association with the parable that follows is a contrivance which actually confuses the original meaning of both passages.

It is verse 15 that explains what gave rise to the telling of the parable. At some time or other, quite unspecified, someone responded to Jesus' preaching of the Kingdom with the pious exclamation: 'Happy the one who will share some day in the feast of the Kingdom of God!' It was the kind of remark that was liable, it seems, to provoke a rather curt, down-to-earth retort from Jesus; as when the sentimental lady interrupted his teaching with: 'My, what a lucky woman your mother was!' 'Blest is the womb that carried you and the breasts you sucked!', and he answered,

'Blest, rather, are the ones who hear God's word and keep it' – which was, incidentally, a pretty perceptive comment on his mother (Luke 11.27,28). In this instance Jesus must have detected in the sanctimonious bystander's interjection about the joys of the heavenly banquet that common belief in a sweet bye and bye that makes no impact on the sweet here and now. So he rounds on him with this story. 'A man once gave a great banquet' – not a king this time, nor a wedding; nothing symbolical in the characters; just an anecdote with a rather unusual twist at the end. Many invitations were given and presumably accepted. The day arrived and, as has already been explained, the courtesy was observed of sending servants round to all the guests to tell them the feast was ready. In those days, and even today in parts of the East, hospitality was leisurely and casual. The chief meal of the day began in the late hours of the afternoon and went on, particularly if it were a special feast, until midnight or after. Though it may have started earlier, it would not have really got going before sunset, and as has already been noted, guests were not expected to arrive all together at the same time. So those who heard Jesus telling this story would not have taken the excuses given through the servant as refusals, but simply as apologies for having to arrive late. Two of them were in the middle of business transactions that they wanted to complete before sundown, and the third, recently married, was presumably observing a Levitical prohibition which lasted until sunset (Lev. 15.16–18). According to those who have made careful study of the Jewish Talmud, etiquette allowed guests to arrive up to the end of the first full course of the meal, though this did convey some degree of disrespect. The point of the story is that this particular host is not prepared to put up with such casualness and decides to teach the late-comers a lesson. He sends his servant into the streets and roads to round up enough people to ensure that, when the late-comers turn up, there will be no room and no supper for them. That is the punch line. What Jesus is saying is, 'Don't make little speeches about future joys, and don't sing hymns about the Kingdom as though there's all the time in the world before it will happen. The guests are already arriving, and eating tomorrow's bread today. You're in danger of being too late.'

It seems most probable that this was the single powerful message that Jesus was giving when he originally told the story. Did it always contain the reference to the poor, the mutilated, the lame, the blind? That introduces a second theme, and Jesus liked to tell stories with just one. The Matthew version does not mention the poor and disabled, and their appearance in the previous paragraph of this chapter suggests that it was the Evangelist himself who was at pains to introduce the poor, the mutilated, the lame, the blind at this point. Yet, on balance, it makes good sense to suppose they were part of the original parable, not as a call for compassion but to explain why the Pharisees and other religious groups could not recognize that the future had started to reach into the present. The banquet of God's kingdom had begun, and the places at the table were being filled by the little people – the poor, the mutilated, the lame and the blind – the very ones whom the ecclesiastics and moralists considered beyond the pale. No wonder they failed to see that the guests were already arriving for God's feast, since these were the last people they expected to find there.

The detailed study of this parable in both its versions opens up the wider question about the huge significance Jesus attached to this image of the celebration-banquet as a symbol and sign of the nearness of God and his sovereignty. It recurs again and again. Only in the Dead Sea Scrolls do we find such emphasis on the banquet theme. In the Qumran community, members of the Council in good standing shared a ritual meal at which the blessing of bread and new wine foreshadowed an equally formalized feast presided over by the two Essene Messiahs.[4]

The Gospel of John opens the Galilean ministry with a wedding feast when new wine is served to the guests; it ends its story, back in Galilee, with a breakfast of bread and fish on the lake shore when a new start is offered to a failed disciple. The one celebrates the start, the other the culmination, of God's redeeming break-through. The same glad gratitude for God's victory marks a similar pairing in the Synoptic Gospels. Early in the Capernaum ministry comes the feast that Levi the tax-gatherer lays on in his home to celebrate the start of a new life; and in the Gospel of Luke this is matched, at the end of the long journey southwards, by the dinner at the house of another tax-gatherer, Zacchaeus. Both these emphasize not only the celebration of God's saving intervention, but the acceptance of the unacceptable within the divine hospitality. But Jesus did not limit his contacts to the poor and outcast. So we have another pair of meals in the homes of Pharisees, both fraught with criticism. The first was the occasion when the woman of the city wept over the feet of Jesus and anointed them with ointment; and, at the second, a man suffering from dropsy was set before him as a trap to see if he would heal him, as it was the Sabbath. At both these meals it is the hosts who seem to stand condemned. They seek the Kingdom through their moral achievement, while he witnesses to a Kingdom *given* to the poor, the mutilated, the lame, the blind. Then, set in the centre of each of the Gospels, is the feeding of the hungry multitude, the sheep without a shepherd, told in an almost ritualistic way as a re-enactment of the provision of manna in the wilderness, and also of the future eschatological banquet. It seems almost certain that Jesus turned that event, whatever it was that actually happened, into a sign, a representation of the banquet of the coming Kingdom, offered before the time to the simple and needy. The Gospel of John says that afterwards there was talk of making him king; in the Gospel of Mark there is the cryptic conversation in the boat, when Jesus makes his disciples

83

recall the details of both occasions when a multitude was fed, and adds emphatically: 'Do you not yet understand?' And, as if to underline the crucial significance of that merciful and heavenly meal for the poor, Mark, followed by Matthew, places it immediately next to its Satanic counter-part, King Herod's birthday banquet for his courtiers and officers which ended in cruelty and death. It is the Devil's misfortune always to be used as a foil to make God's point, the fall-guy in the divine comedy.

To call these and other actions of Jesus 'acted parables' is a helpful insight; he saw significance in them, as he saw it in the incidents he narrated as parables. But this ought not to imply that he went about setting up such performances as object lessons comparable to his taking a child or washing the disciples' feet. On all these occasions the most natural interpretation of the text is that he was making a spontane-ous response to a human situation – at the celebration in Levi's home, the encounter with Zacchaeus, the meals in the homes of his critics, the feeding of the multitude and, in the Gospel of John, the wedding at Cana and the breakfast on the lake shore. These events were for Jesus a matter of doing what he saw the Father doing, treating people as he saw God treating people, good and bad alike. Purely on that score he saw all those meals as a deliberate anticipation of the eschatological feast, sharing tomorrow's bread today. That was precisely, and most deliberately of all, what he intended by the meal that he planned on the night before his death. The sharing of the bread and the cup of wine on that occasion was a means of sealing an unbreakable unity between Jesus and his companions; it also offered to them a participation in his surrender of life and the benefits procured by it; but, supremely among all the other meals to which the Gospels draw attention, it was a prior realization of the banquet of the Kingdom of God in advance of its universal fulfilment. Every account of the institution of the eucharist in the New Testament contains, in one form or another, a clear reference to the coming new age. 'Take and eat this . . . Drink this, all of you', is an invitation to take tomorrow's bread today, with all the boldness and risk that this entails.

Apart from the faith which boldness and risk require, the invitation is unconditional. That truth emerges from understanding the Last Supper in the context of those other meals in the Gospels. There had been more to those meals than including the poor and the disadvantaged. They were sinners, and not only in the eyes of the most extreme *Chaberim*. The Gospel of Mark says on its own account: 'As he reclined at table in Levi's house, many tax-collectors and sinners were reclining with Jesus and his disciples.' They were the friends and associates of Levi's old way of life; he'd had no time to make new ones, nor is there any indication that Jesus asked that of him. Many of them, says the Gospel, were followers of Jesus; yet it calls them sinners. Admittedly the word refers as much to neglect of the ritual as of the moral code. But that does not apply in the case of Zacchaeus, who admitted to fraud and extortion, nor to the woman of the city, who came uninvited to that other dinner party to anoint the feet of Jesus, of whom the host on that occasion thought to himself, 'If this man were a prophet, he would have known what sort of woman this is who is touching him; for she is a sinner.'

Christian moralists usually get round the embarrassment of all these sinners in the company of Jesus by assuming that they had repented and given up their sin. Broadly speaking that may have been true, or at least the process of turning around had begun. Many of Levi's companions had started to follow Jesus, the woman of the city was weeping as she anointed his feet, and Zacchaeus promised full restitution. But if that were the general rule in the case of the people Jesus accepted, most of the Pharisees would have had no problem with him. They too thought it was a good work to bring a sinner to repentance, and, if repentant, then they

85

were no longer sinners. So why shouldn't Jesus welcome them? His detractors must have had more solid grounds for their censures than that. In their eyes Jesus would have appeared pastorally too happy-go-lucky. He seems to have said very little about repentance, compared with John the Baptist. The Pharisees would have agreed with John, for he had said, 'Prove your repentance by the fruit it bears. It is not enough to panic because you hear rumours of doom.' It takes time to test the permanence of a conversion and there ought to be some change of life-style. But Jesus was altogether too hasty in his acceptance of such people. Before Zacchaeus had said a word about restitution or shown the slightest contrition, Jesus had invited himself to dinner. Surely they were justified in saying, 'He has gone to be the guest of a sinner.' They could not see that a man who has already laid aside sin and made good the past is no longer a sinner; what he needs is not forgiveness, but recognition. Forgiveness has to be premature or it is not forgiveness. Grace cannot wait and see. It acts as though the relationship were already made good, even before that has happened. In this it mirrors the prematurity of those who live the life of the Kingdom even before it has arrived.

Whoever is fool enough to trust unilaterally and accept unconditionally is taking the same gamble as the one who included Judas Iscariot and Simon Peter in the invitation to share in the bread and the cup. In the same spirit of inclusiveness Jesus recognized the incipient response of some non-Jews and prophesied, 'I tell you many will come from east and west and recline at table in the Kingdom of heaven with Abraham, Isaac and Jacob, while the children of the Kingdom will be turned out into the dark.' That began to happen within a few years of the resurrection of Jesus, and at once the church was divided between those who wanted the Gentiles to prove their conversion by submitting to the Jewish way of life, and those who felt they must embrace them as Gentiles just as they were, with only a minimal basis of conformity. It was the latter who were living the life of the future rule of God in advance of its arrival. They were taking hold of the new age in which there will no longer be any rights or any claims, no question of repayments or deserts. Those things belong to the totality of values by which the present age lives, values which the present age regards as infallible. They are the moral framework of the world we know, which cannot cancel debts but, like avarice personified, can only conceive of advancing further loans so that the interest shall be paid and paid again to the uttermost farthing. That moneylenders' code, which is called good business, is closely related to the ethics of rights and deserts, which is called good morality. But the age that regards both those codes as axiomatic is passing. It is self-excluded from the prayer 'Forgive us our debts as we herewith forgive our debtors.' For that prayer, like the petitions that precede it in the Lord's Prayer, is also pleading here and now for something that belongs to the future age of God's perfect sovereignty, when the victory over evil will have been won, the judgment pronounced, and all things reconciled.

Jesus was not indifferent to morality and goodness. He looked for a righteousness that went beyond that of the Pharisees. But he never made that a precondition of his welcome. This was the point of his greatest banquet story. There was nothing in the repentance of the Prodigal Son to disturb the established order. He fulfilled the Jewish proverb, 'When the Israelites are short of beans they return to God.' The young son understands that if he is allowed back he must prove himself by working for his keep. It is the father's impetuous behaviour that rocks the moral foundations. He asks for no test of genuineness, receives his son as an honoured guest, and hands back at once the ring of authority in the management of the farm. And the climax, the thing that scandalizes and upsets the elder brother, is that such an extravagant feast should be laid on for such a cause. But to the father there can be no better cause: 'He who was lost is found; he who was dead, is alive. How can we help celebrating?' That is going to be the motive and the theme of the triumphant Feast of Fools at the end of all things. It should be the motive and the theme of every act of inclusion and forgiveness by which we anticipate that future and make tomorrow ours today.

SIX

The Narrow Road

17 And as he was setting out on his journey, a man ran up and knelt before him, and asked him, 'Good Teacher, what must I do to inherit eternal life?' [18]And Jesus said to him, 'Why do you call me good? No one is good but God alone. [19]You know the commandments: "Do not kill, Do not commit adultery, Do not steal, Do not bear false witness, Do not defraud, Honour your father and mother."' [20]And he said to him, 'Teacher, all these I have observed from my youth.' [21]And Jesus looking upon him loved him, and said to him, 'You lack one thing; go, sell what you have, and give to the poor, and you will have treasure in heaven; and come, follow me.' [22]At that saying his countenance fell, and he went away sorrowful; for he had great possessions.

23 And Jesus looked around and said to his disciples, 'How hard it will be for those who have riches to enter the kingdom of God!' [24]And the disciples were amazed at his words. But Jesus said to them again, 'Children, how hard it is to enter the kingdom of God! [25]It is easier for a camel to go through the eye of a needle than for a rich man to enter the kingdom of God.' [26]And they were exceedingly astonished, and said to him, 'Then who can be saved?' [27]Jesus looked at them and said, 'With men it is impossible, but not with God; for all things are possible with God.' [28]Peter began to say to him, 'Lo, we have left everything and followed you.' [29]Jesus said, 'Truly, I say to you, there is no one who has left house or brothers or sisters or mother or father or children or lands, for my sake and for the gospel, [30]who will not receive a hundredfold now in this time, houses and brothers and sisters and mothers and children and lands, with persecutions, and in the age to come eternal life. [31]But many that are first will be last, and the last first.'

32 And they were on the road, going up to Jerusalem, and Jesus was walking ahead of them; and they were amazed, and those who followed

were afraid. And taking the twelve again, he began to tell them what was to happen to him, ³³*saying, 'Behold, we are going up to Jerusalem; and the Son of man will be delivered to the chief priests and the scribes, and they will condemn him to death, and deliver him to the Gentiles;* ³⁴*and they will mock him, and spit upon him, and scourge him, and kill him; and after three days he will rise.'*

35 And James and John, the sons of Zeb'edee, came forward to him, and said to him, 'Teacher, we want you to do for us whatever we ask of you.' ³⁶*And he said to them, 'What do you want me to do for you?'* ³⁷*And they said to him, 'Grant us to sit, one at your right hand and one at your left, in your glory.'* ³⁸*But Jesus said to them, 'You do not know what you are asking. Are you able to drink the cup that I drink, or to be baptized with the baptism with which I am baptized?'* ³⁹*And they said to him, 'We are able.' And Jesus said to them, 'The cup that I drink you will drink; and with the baptism with which I am baptized, you will be baptized;* ⁴⁰*but to sit at my right hand or at my left is not mine to grant, but it is for those for whom it has been prepared.'* ⁴¹*And when the ten heard it, they began to be indignant at James and John.* ⁴²*And Jesus called them to him and said to them, 'You know that those who are supposed to rule over the Gentiles lord it over them, and their great men exercise authority over them.* ⁴³*But it shall not be so among you; but whoever would be great among you must be your servant,* ⁴⁴*and whoever would be first among you must be slave of all.* ⁴⁵*For the Son of man also came not to be served but to serve, and to give his life as a ransom for many.'*

Mark 10.17–45

Human nature being what it is, one might surmise that a large part of the anger of the elder brother in the parable of the Prodigal son was prompted, though he would not have admitted it, by his belief that his father was making a fool of himself, and not for the first time either. The stories Jesus told are rich in characters who must have caused acute embarrassment to their more sensible children – the vineyard owner who paid the same wage for an hour as for a day, the woman who set about mixing half a hundred-weight of dough, the head of state who coolly wrote off a bad debt of millions, or the jeweller who traded his entire stock for one stone. Jesus appears to have had a particular fondness for such immoderate personalities, choosing as the ultimate leader of his apostles the one who, they said, was rash enough to try walking on the water. Jesus shared a natural affinity with the kind of extravagant spontaneity that does not, on the whole, commend a person for preferment in the church in these days. But then he was looking for followers who could respond as he was responding to the nearness of God and the sovereignty of God in this world. He was one whose own family said he was out of his mind (Mark 3.21, NEB), and it could be said, therefore, that Paul won the highest accolade as a Christian when the Roman procurator, Festus, shouted him down, saying, 'Paul, you are raving; too much study is driving you mad' (Acts 26.24). Writing to the Corinthian church some four years earlier, Paul had declared, 'We are fools for Christ's sake', and, 'If anyone among you fancies himself wise according to the values of this passing age, let him become a fool to gain true wisdom' (I Cor. 3.18; 4.10).

There is much to be said for the position of the court jester in the Middle Ages. There have been illustrious names among the wearers of the cap and bells. Rahere, who was Fool to Henry I, founded St Bartholomew's Hospital. Malory recalled that King Arthur was provided with a jester called Dagonet, who was knighted for his services. Henry VIII had two notable clowns in attendance, one of them a woman. The last Fool to grace the English court was probably Charles I's Muckle John, but in France the famous L'Angely could still 'set the table on a roar' through most of the reign of Louis XVI. Everyone treated the jester as a joke, yet with faintly superstitious attention, since one who was a bit 'touched' might speak as an oracle. For these reasons the Fool could often get away with telling the monarch those home-truths no one else dared put into words, though he could easily be ignored as a harmless buffoon, or whipped and sent to the pillory if his jokes struck too near the bone. Francis of Assisi understood this role very well when he called himself and his friars 'God's jesters', and he demonstrated the innocent power of a fool for Christ in that age of the Crusades when he passed unarmed through the Saracen lines around Damietta, with a bounty on his Christian head, and had days of courteous religious discourse with the dreaded Sultan, Malik-al-Kamil.

When the age of reason overtook the ages of faith, the more flattering black page-boys displaced the jesters from the royal palaces of Europe, and the latter went on holding up the mirror of truth in the more plebeian guise of clowns and punchinellos. Even in the most repressive periods of Stalin's rule, the miniature comedians of the Russian puppet-theatres continued their mockeries unscathed when all other critics had been muzzled. So it is neither shocking nor surprising that Georges Rouault and other artists of this century should have portrayed Christ as a gentle, suffering clown. For in Galilee, and ever since, he has been gathering around himself a growing company of men and women whose stock in trade is a kind of defiant absurdity, the absurdity of behaving openly as though they are living in a different world from this, under a different regime, with quite different assumptions.

The most natural reaction to such a movement, either in Jesus' own day or in the modern world, would be to dismiss it as a harmless lunacy, like the bands of extreme millenialists who sat on mountain tops to await the end of the world on a particular date. But what Jesus started has proved to be more subversive than that. For the witness of people who have the gall to live as though God's future were already reaching into the present sets up a sign of that future which continues to haunt even those who reject it as unrealistic.

The brave demonstration of those Arab and Israeli families who share a common life in their Oasis of Peace does not appear to have affected the course of events in that tragic land. Yet in the spring of 1987, when the young Jews and Arabs who had attended their peace-training courses were invited with their families to a reunion, twenty thousand came to that bleak hillside on a Saturday to celebrate an alternative way forward.

Forgiveness is not widely regarded as a force to be reckoned with in Northern Ireland; yet when one man testified to his freedom from bitterness towards the perpetrators of the bombing at the Inniskillen Armistice Day parade, in which his daughter died, a whole sceptical society was taken aback as though it had been presented for one moment with a completely new option. Such glimpses stick in the mind like the memory of a signpost pointing to an alternative route, which one did not risk at the time because it looked such a minor road.

The Scottish poet Edwin Muir perceived that a much-quoted saying of Jesus is a parable of the Kingdom in this sense.

The great road stretched before them, clear and still,
Then from in front one cried: 'Turn back! Turn back!'
Yet they had never seen so fine a track,
Honest and frank past any thought of ill.
But when they glanced behind, how strange, how strange,
These wild demented windings in and out –
Traced by some devil of mischief or of doubt? –
That was the road they had come by. Could it change?

How could they penetrate that perilous maze
Backwards, again, climb backwards down the scree
From the wrong side, slither among the dead?
Yet as they travelled on, for many days
These words rang in their ears as if they said,
'There was another road you did not see.'[1]

Very often the preaching and the living of the Kingdom amounts to no more than that. It is a sign-post.

An instructive example of the contribution of the jester at court was provided during the national coal strike of 1986 by an episode almost unknown to the public, though the main protagonists were aware of it. It is best told in the words of one of the chaplains in the Glamorgan Industrial Mission, somewhat abbreviated.

'We sat like schoolboys in the front desks of the NUM board room in Pontypridd: a provincial moderator of the United Reformed Church, the General Secretary of the Council of Churches for Wales, the minister of a Welsh chapel in the Rhondda, and an industrial chaplain. *They* sat looking down from their high table with benevolent scepticism: the officers of the South Wales Area of the NUM and a couple of miners' agents.

'The initiative had been taken by the minister of the chapel. Our team of four had come quickly together to determine whether anything could be done. We were looking for common ground between both sides in Wales, and for an approach that might stimulate from within Wales some movement back to the negotiating table in both London and Sheffield. On neither side did the top leadership seem interested in negotiation. In almost every coalfield the drift back to work had started, except in South Wales where loyalty to the Union was solid.

'The South Wales NUM President received us courteously, but his words were patronizing and profoundly sceptical. For half an hour the conversation centred upon the solidarity of the South Wales miners. Then came our question: "South Wales solidarity is about the only card left in the NUM pack; but how will you play it? Too soon, and the comrades in Sheffield will accuse you of breaking the strike; hold on too long, and it will be too late to play it." Our question changed the whole atmosphere. We were no longer a quartet of well-meaning parsons. Naïve we might be, but informed; and probably trustworthy. We just might be able to help. "Go and talk to Phil

Weekes, the Coal Board Area Director," they said, "and come back to us."

'This was a pattern repeated throughout our involvement: in the initial meeting the same day with the Area Director, in subsequent meetings with him and senior staff of ACAS in London, and with Ian MacGregor and NCB managers and directors in Hobart House. It was only when we had demonstrated that we had done our homework and were aware of the details of negotiating positions and the political stances underlying the issues, that we could put our apparently naïve questions. By keeping the low profile and low-ranking status of our position we were, perhaps, able to exercise a freedom and a kind of "spiritual" authority which is still recognized in the industrial society. But we were never so naïve as to be unaware of the way we might be manipulated and used.'

It is no longer germane to outline the proposal they worked out through these many meetings. It was calculated to appeal to the many more moderate minds on both sides, and it attracted growing interest in some of the national dailies. The Welsh church leaders, Free Church, Anglican and Catholic, co-ordinated their more high-profile representations with the unobtrusive spade-work of the team of four in a well-planned strategy. It looked as though they just might succeed when, unhappily, the game was snatched from their jesters' hands by more prestigious courtiers from the church and the TUC, both outside Wales. The weakness, but also the strange strength of the clown, lies in the fact that he can so easily be up-staged. It looked, and felt, like failure – yet not entirely. For a few people had caught sight of a possible alternative that would not go away, even though rejected. The ultimately subversive question had been planted: 'Do things really have to be like this?' That is the gift which those who dare to live God's future now offer to the world. They are God's clowns, juggling question-marks. Their audience can never again

95

say with the old confidence that they had 'no alternative', and a door has been thrown open to God and his infinite possibilities.

Again and again, it seems from the gospels, various interests asked Jesus to give them a sign, unaware that he was doing just that. The only sign he had to give them to show that the age of God's perfect sovereignty was at hand was himself, and those who, with him, were living the life of that future. 'For just as Jonah was a sign to the Ninevites' – albeit a most reluctant sign of God's *chesed*, his compassion and constancy – 'so will the Son of Man be to this generation' (Luke 11.30; Jonah 4.2). One who glimpsed the alternative to which that sign pointed was the wealthy man whose hunger for the life of the ages, the life of the future, set him running to intercept Jesus (Mark 10.17–22).

'Good Teacher, what must I do?'

'It is not good teachers you need. God is the one you must deal with, and you can go to him direct: you know his commandments.'

'I have observed them since my youth – difficult, but possible, reasonable.'

'Well then, try something unreasonable. Sell up those possessions and give away your wealth and find the treasure God has for you.'

He could see the alternative road set before his very eyes: those shabby men and women around Jesus had taken it. Perhaps it was not his wealth that held him back, so much as the impossibility of making a fool of himself. Rich people find it very hard to break rank. Only the fools are free.

Jesus loved the rich man. His unconditional acceptance of people was not limited to the poor and the rejects. He dined with Pharisees as well as tax-gatherers, and in his story the Father goes out to the elder son as well as the younger. As the sad stranger walked away, Jesus looked around at the little band of followers who had started along the narrow alternative road with him. It hadn't been so hard for them to feel the pull of God's future and start living it now; they had not got so much invested in the present. Those who have plenty have less edge to their appetite for a new world. And now, here was Peter, boasting of the choice they had made: 'Look, we have left everything and followed you.' The text says Peter *began* to say this, so it sounds as though he intended to go on for some time! Jesus cut in. Yes, this *was* true. Their boats and fishing gear, their house on the Capernaum waterfront and the plot of land on the hill, might be worth less than the rich man spent on a single dinner party. But they had left their families, too; and, as Peter said, they had left all – their earlier assumptions and loyalties and expectations. They had taken to an entirely new way of thinking that reflected the mind of the Father and his sovereignty. They were the first-fruits of a new creation. These men and women, who had caught from Jesus a sense of the nearness of God, and had dared with him to take hold of the future now, were the seed he had come to sow, the leaven in the dough of the world. These were the ones to whom the Father was delighted to 'give' the Kingdom. They, together with Jesus, were to be that 'Son of Man', that mysterious figure in the visions of the Book of Daniel who is both singular and plural, to whom the Ancient of Days was seen giving the Kingdom that would never pass away.

Libraries of books have been written on the meaning of that title which Jesus seems to have taken to himself. It is a phrase that had been used with several connotations, and must have resonated with all of them to a greater or lesser degree by the time Jesus used it. That he did use it seems probable from the fact that it appears frequently in the Gospels, including that of John, but nowhere else in the New Testament, except for one quotation from Psalm 8 and three deliberate echoes from the vision of Daniel 7 (Heb. 2.6; Acts 7.56; Rev. 1.13; 14.14). There is no evidence that the title 'Son of Man' was first applied to Jesus by the early church as a development of its teaching; and the only reason for its frequent use in the Gospels is the strength of the tradition that Jesus himself used it.

But what did he mean by it? As a common Aramaic term, based on Old Testament Hebrew, it could mean simply humanity as such, as in the poetic reiteration of Psalm 8.4. In that simple sense Jesus might have taken it as a title signifying 'I, as man' or 'I, as the true self of the human race'.[2] If 'Son of Man' bears this representative meaning, then it accords with the Pauline teaching about Christ as the 'last Adam', the 'second Man'. Some of those taking this stance have also pointed out that the biblical use of the phrase 'Son of Man' usually sounds an overtone of pathos for human mortality. It means 'mortal man', humanity in its weakness and vulnerability.[3] That additional reverberation would have drawn Jesus to adopt the title if, as seems likely, he had begun to identify the kingly Messiah with the suffering Servant of Yahweh.[4]

But if he was thinking of his special role in relation to the nearness of God and his sovereignty in these terms of Messiahship at all, Jesus must have associated his chosen self-designation as 'Son of Man' with the eschatological significance those words had derived from the Book of Daniel, subsequently elaborated in those parts of the Book of Enoch which were circulating in his time. Professor C. F. D. Moule has held firmly to the opinion that the form of the title which occurs in the Gospels means '*that* Son of Man', and is intended as a reference back to Daniel 7 as it stood in Jesus' day.[5] In the account of his trial, he answered the High Priest's question, Are you Messiah?, by speaking of the Son of Man. Now, it has been noted several times in this book that the image of the 'one like unto a Son of Man', coming with the clouds of heaven, who was presented to the Ancient of Days, merges into that of the holy ones of the Most High to whom, after their tribulation, 'shall be given the kingly power and sovereignty and greatness of all the kingdoms under heaven'. The Gospels record Jesus as speaking of himself sometimes as 'I', sometimes as 'the Son of Man'. Occasionally he draws a distinction between them: 'Whoever is ashamed of me and of my words in this adulterous and sinful generation, of him will the Son of Man also be ashamed when he comes in the glory of his Father with the holy angels' (Mark 8.38). It may be that the distinction is precisely that which the Book of Enoch draws between 'the Son of Man without power' and 'the Son of Man with power'. But it is a more consistent reading of the texts to deduce that when Jesus says 'Son of Man' he usually means himself together with those who are committed to living out the sovereignty of their Father. It is he and they together, who live the future Kingdom now, who, as Son of Man, have authority to forgive sins. It is they and he together who in freedom took and ate the ears of corn, who, as Son of Man, were Lord of the Sabbath. And now he takes the twelve, his representatives of the new Israel of the future, and says, 'Behold, we are going up to Jerusalem, and the Son of Man will be handed over to the chief priests and scribes, and they will condemn him to death and hand him over to the Gentiles, who will mock him and spit upon him and scourge him and kill him, and after three days he will rise' (Mark 10.32–34).

Did Jesus really believe that those who were one with him in knowing God as their Abba, and one with him in reflecting the character of that God in their relationships, and one with him in living the life of the future sovereignty of that God as though it had already broken into the present, would also be one with him in the suffering and the death and the consummation beyond death? It seems that, at least for part of the time, that was in his mind. When he said on more than one occasion, 'Whoever wants to be my follower' – not just a listener-disciple – 'must leave self, take up his cross and come with me', the trivial use of those words as a metaphor had not been developed. In a saying that both Matthew and Luke record, though with variants, he said: 'You are those who have stood firmly with me in my trials; and now I vest in you the Kingship which my Father vested in me; you shall eat and drink at my table in my Kingdom and sit on thrones as judges of the twelve tribes of Israel' (Luke 22.28–30). His ultimate confidence in the corporate reality of the 'Son of Man' was not shaken even by the continuing misconceptions of the men he had chosen to share the enterprise most intimately with him. Blind as they were, this insistent hope of Jesus was the germ of the future doctrine of the church as the Body of Christ.

'And James and John, the sons of Zebedee, came forward to him. "Master, we want you to do for us whatever we ask of you." "What do you want me to do for you?" "Grant us to sit, one on your right and one on your left in your glory."'

So that was how they envisaged the immediate course of events: up to Jerusalem, some kind of show-down, and then the start of the Messianic reign! Such a gulf of misunderstanding must have dashed his hopes of sharing it all with them. 'Jesus said to them, "You do not know what you are asking. Are you able to drink the cup that I drink, or to be baptized with the baptism with which I am baptized?"' According to the Synoptic Gospels the metaphors of cup and baptism were part of Jesus' own thinking. 'I came to cast fire upon the earth, and how I wish it were already alight! I have a baptism to undergo, and how weighed down I am until it is over' (Luke 12.50); and in Gethsemane he was going to pray that the cup might pass him by. This is an aspect of the two major sacraments – communion with him at the ultimate depth – which an easy-going church often ignores, but which may have been of central significance for him. For when he passed the cup to them at the supper table – 'This is my blood of the covenant, poured out for the many' – was he not inviting them and us to share his dying? And when the Fourth Gospel deliberately substitutes the feet-washing for the institution of the eucharist in the upper room, was it not a symbolic invitation and opportunity for them to share the baptism he must undergo – 'If I do not wash you, you have no part, no share, in me'? James and John, at any rate, dimly understood what he was saying now. 'We can do it.' Jesus accepted the avowal. 'The cup that I drink, you will drink, and the baptism I am baptized with shall be yours. But sitting on my right and my left is not for me to grant.' Their unreadiness to be one with him in the ordeal is only a postponement. The Gospel of John, as so often, has words that sing the same tune as the Synoptists: 'Where I am going you cannot follow me now, but one day you will' (John 13.36).

But what has this certainty of death got to do with the Kingdom? Or, in other words, why was it that Jesus, whose whole message and mission was concentrated upon the sovereignty of his Father and its imminent fulfilment, had to die?

To ask why anyone died is to ask two questions which are quite distinct: what caused the death, and what was the purpose of it? Or, if the second question sounds too high-flown for an event so natural and universal, what brought it about, and what did she or he make of it? In the case of Jesus the first of these questions is answered by the whole story of the witness he bore to the truth he knew. He was the one who fitted into none of the existing parties or movements. He was the jester who overstepped the bounds and had to be sent to the pillory. He was the trader in questions that proved subversive, and by living as though the future were here he threatened to unbalance the present. This is what brought about his death, and the deaths of many of his followers since then. But that leaves the further question: when Jesus saw that his death would be inevitable if he persisted, what meaning did he give it, what purpose could he see in it? Like everything else he undertook, the purpose was linked to his understanding of the Kingdom of God.

He had been daring to pray the gifts of the new age into this present world-order, and to grasp those gifts by living the life of the Kingdom, the life that reflected his Father's nature, in anticipation of its full realization on earth. But he understood that, if these prayers were to be answered and the things that belonged to God's future were to be experienced today, he could not pick and choose between them; he must take the rough of tomorrow as well as its smooth. And one inescapable feature of the coming of God's reign, foreseen by most of the prophets and apocalyptists, was the final conflict between God and the concentrated forces of evil. Or, to put it in another way, there could be no entry into a totally new life without a dying of the old, no radical restoration of Israel without an end to Israel, no Kingdom of God without a prior judgment of the powers of this world. This is the theme of the last visionary book of the Bible with its lurid and fantastic images of catastrophe and conflict. It is called The Apocalypse, which means 'the uncovering'. That title points not only to the unveiling of the future, but more specifically to the uncovering or stripping down of all who find themselves caught up in that 'hour of trial which is coming on the whole world, to put to the test those who dwell upon the earth' (Rev. 3.10), so that the naked reality of what each person is and what each institution is in its truth is disclosed. The word *peirasmos* may be used of the commonplace temptations by which the virtue or faithfulness of anyone is put on trial; and the ethical teaching of the Bible is, generally speaking, that this is a necessary and strengthening experience, not one from which a person should pray for exemption. But *peirasmos* may also mean the eschatological ordeal that must prelude the final victory of God and the new age of his perfected sovereignty, and that is quite another matter, from which one may rightly pray, 'Do not bring us to that testing.' The great ordeal is the narrow gate, the constricted passage-way, that leads through to life – for it is significant that in the Gospel of Matthew the epithet used of the alternative road is derived from the same root as the word for the great tribulation.

If tomorrow's bread, the justice and peace of the Kingdom, can be given today, if the forgiveness of the jubilee age to come can be the way of life in the present for those who will accept it, the great ordeal which puts the inner core of individuals and nations to the test must also be confronted in the here and now by those who have dared to live the future now. They, the Son of Man, came not to be served but to serve and to surrender life as a ransom for the many. A ransom is a payment made to win another's freedom or exemption. Jesus undertook to endure the great tribulation of the last days, to be stripped bare and tested by the ordeal on behalf of humanity, to pass through that narrowing-down of all things to the point of extinction, and so win a passage through into a new dimension of life. And he invited those who, with him, were calling that future life into the present to go through with him on behalf of the world.

To face that startling truth does not diminish the uniqueness of Jesus and his sacrifice. It adds to it. Who but God ever desired to share his uniqueness with others? They were not ready to take up the invitation then, but it has never been withdrawn. And one by one, ever since, there have been those who, facing the choice as to what they might make of their death or their affliction or their loss of God, have offered it, like Paul, 'to make up the full tale of Christ's afflictions still to be endured' (Col. 1.24).

For the present, however, he had to enter the ordeal alone. He had already faced such an ordeal when the Spirit moved him to wrestle in the wilderness with the Devil's testing over the meaning of his vocation. Now in his passion he faced an ultimate onslaught. His prayer that the cup might pass away was indeed the cry, 'Do not bring us into the ordeal.' He could not have known to what a strait the narrowing road would bring him. He had lived in the perpetual presence of the God he called Father. For him and with him he could endure the long agony, and he trusted that this God would be with him to the end. Yet in the darkness that was no longer true. If we take the words recorded in the Gospel of Mark as an audible cry rather than the muttered recital of a psalm, he was stripped of everything, even that nearness of God which had given him his vision and his certainty of the Kingdom. Only the reality of his inner truth survived that fire. He had given up everything else.

It was, of course, an ordeal also for those others who had adventured with him up to that point. He had told them, according to the passion story: 'Tonight you will fall from your faith on my account. Stay awake and pray that you may be spared the ordeal' (Matt. 26.31; Luke 22.40). They too were stripped down by it. Peter saw himself with neither strength nor fidelity of his own. All suffered a burden of hopeless guilt, besides their loss of him. There was no more future to be lived in the present. That door had been locked again.

But they were wrong. Up till then their challenge to the world had been a kind of make-believe, just a way of looking at things. Let's pretend with this man Jesus that we are already under God's perfect sovereignty. Let's play Kingdom Come. But that masquerade ended when the costumes had been stripped off. On the third day it started for real. The impossible dream actually happened. In the risen Christ God's future, something that could belong only to the end of time, was brought into the here and now. The Kingdom of the ultimate fulfilment was brought into their midst in the person of this Lord, raised into unprecedented newness of life. In him the Kingdom that is not of this world was laid open to all who believed, and tomorrow's bread was given today, and day by day.

Henceforward, 'as Christ was raised from the dead by the glory of God the Father, we too should walk in newness of life' – living the life of the new age now, openly, boldly, in the whole life of this world. It is for this that the Lord is here. It is for this that his Spirit is with us. 'For, where anyone is united to Christ, there is a new world; the old order has gone. See, the new has begun.'

NOTES

Prelude The Quest

1. Josephus, *Jewish Antiquities*, Loeb Edition, London 1965, XVIII.3.3; cf. XVIII.1.1 and 5.2, XX.5.1; and *Wars* II.13.2.

One The Authentic Voice

1. See, as abbreviated examples, Acts 10.37–43; 13.17–41.
2. I Cor. 7.10; 9.14; 11.23–25; 15.3–9; Rom. 14.14; I Thess. 4.8; 5.2–6; James 1.22; 3.12; 5.12.
3. Eusebius, *Ecclesiastical History*, Penguin Classics Edition 1965, p. 152.
4. John A. T. Robinson, *Twelve More New Testament Studies*, SCM Press 1984, pp. 27–31.
5. X. Léon-Dufour, *The Gospels and the Jesus of History*, Collins 1968, pp. 109–113; John A. T. Robinson, *Redating the New Testament*, SCM Press 1976, p. 101; C. H. Dodd, *The Founder of Christianity*, Collins 1970, p. 19.
6. If this is the case, it conforms with the tradition, reported by Bishop Papias of Hierapolis early in the second century, that Mark, while in Rome with Peter, wrote down, just as he heard them, the anecdotes which the apostle recounted in the course of his teaching. Whether that became the more primitive narrative on which all three Evangelists relied or was the first draft of our second Gospel is still a matter of debate. In its present form that Gospel is not the artless, rough-hewn account that its style has led people to suppose; there are many subtleties in its composition. Moreover, a letter of Clement of Alexandria which came to light in the early 1970s claims that Mark withheld from the Gospel as we have it certain incidents related to Jesus' practice of initiating new followers in secret, but divulged these 'mysteries' later in a fuller version. See C. H. Dodd, op. cit, pp. 24 f.; J. A. T. Robinson, *Redating the New Testament*, p. 109 n.; F. Kermode, *The Genesis of Secrecy*, Harvard University Press 1979, pp. 57 f.
7. Marion L. Soards, *The Passion according to Luke*, JSOT Press, Sheffield 1987, pp. 124 f.; X. Léon-Dufour, op. cit. pp. 142–145.
8. Stephen Smalley, *John: Evangelist and Interpreter*, Paternoster

107

Press 1978, pp. 41–84; B. E. Westcott, *The Gospel according to St John*, Murray 1882, pp. x-xviii; C. H. Dodd, op. cit., pp. 22 f.

9. The phrase occurs thirteen times in the Gospel of Mark and is retained in nine of the parallel passages in Matthew, but in only three of them in Luke. The Gospel of Matthew twice adds the phrase to its version of a Markan text which does not contain it. In seven, possibly eight, non-Markan passages common to the two other Synoptists, Matthew includes the phrase, while Luke does not. But the fact that in five of these instances Luke inserts a different but similar word, such as 'truly' or 'certainly', suggests that the 'Amen' was there in the common source. Obviously the phrase appealed to the compiler of Matthew's Gospel; it occurs thirteen times in the material peculiar to that book. Possibly he read into the words some such claim to a divine mandate as the 'Thus saith the Lord' of the Old Testament prophets. It is equally clear that the Gospel of Luke prefers to avoid the Hebrew-Aramaic phrase, presumably out of consideration for Gentile readers, yet even so it appears three times in the purely Lukan material.

10. C. F. Burney, *The Poetry of Our Lord*, OUP 1925; J. Jeremias, *The Prayers of Jesus*, SCM Press 1967.

11. Eta Linnemann, *Parables of Jesus: Introduction and Exposition*, SPCK 1966, pp. 3–8.

Two Expectation in the Air

1. G. Ernest Wright, *The Old Testament against its Environment*, SCM Press 1950, p. 23.

2. For a fuller treatment of this social ethic, see my *Enough is Enough*, SCM Press 1975, ch. 3.

3. Scholars disagree as to the exact religious significance that was attributed to the Davidic Kingship. In Egypt the Pharaoh was regarded as the incarnation of the sun-god, Horus, but in northern Mesopotamia kings were only the human viceroys of the god. Kingship would probably have been a largely secular institution in Hebrew society had David not established himself in Jerusalem, where there was already a cult of priest-kings looking back to Melchizedek. Psalms such as 72 and 110 appear to attribute a mythical origin and power to the monarch, so it has been suggested that in Jerusalem the king played a central role in the liturgical presentations of Yahweh's victorious enthronement. This does seem far-fetched in face of the strict ban on imaging God, and the absence of any prophetic criticism of the kings of Judah on that score. More influential in shaping Judaism's messianic expectations was the record of the promise conveyed through the prophet Nathan in II Sam. 7 that the Davidic dynasty would last

indefinitely and bring peace and prosperity to the kingdom. The recollection of such a promise was naturally revived at the birth or the anointing of each new king in Jerusalem, and this may have occasioned some of the messianic prophecies of Isaiah (9 and 11). See Edmond Jacob, *The Theology of the Old Testament*, Hodder and Stoughton 1958, pp. 327–337, and G. Ernest Wright, op. cit., pp. 63–68.

4. Josephus, *Antiquities*, xiii.288,298; xviii.15

5. Emil Schürer, *The History of the Jewish People in the time of Jesus Christ* (ed. Geza Vermes, Fergus Miller and Matthew Black), Vol. II, T. & T. Clark 1979, p. 464, n. 1.

6. For a fuller discussion of this unresolved argument see Joachim Jeremias, *Jerusalem in the Time of Jesus*, SCM Press 1969, ch. XI; John Bowker, *Jesus and the Pharisees*, CUP 1973, pp. 1–42 and relevant quotations; E. P. Sanders, *Jesus and Judaism*, SCM Press 1985, Introduction and ch. 6.

Interlude   Where does he Stand?

1. E. P. Sanders, *Jesus and Judaism*, SCM Press 1985. But see also J. Bowker, *Jesus and the Pharisees*, CUP 1973.

2. Katherine Folliot, *Jesus before he was God*, H. & B. Publications, Richmond, Surrey 1978.

3. D. W. Ferm (ed.) *Third World Liberation Theologies*, Orbis Books, Maryknoll 1986. For further light on the plausibility of this view see Gerd Theissen, *The Shadow of the Galilean*, SCM Press 1987.

4. Matt. 9.14; 14.1; Mark 3.22; 7.1–5; 8.11; 12; 13; Luke 14.1; 20.20– 26.

Three   How Soon is Quickly?

1. Aboth ii.6. Quoted in Hastings' *Dictionary of the Bible*, Vol. III, art. 'Pharisees', p. 827.

2. Joachim Jeremias, *Jerusalem in the Time of Jesus*, gives detailed lists of despised trades in ch. XIV. Most of his evidence belongs to the second century AD, but the reproach must have originated earlier, especially in the case of tax-gatherers, moneylenders, tanners, and businesses notorious for sharp practice.

3. Joachim Jeremias, *The Parables of Jesus* (revd edn), SCM Press 1963, p. 153.

4. Some commentators have interpreted verse 21 in exactly the same sense as verse 24: 'Before you can say "Here it comes!" it's upon you.' But this is a very strained translation of the Greek or of any Aramaic equivalent. The Greek *entos* means 'on the inside'.

5. For this understanding of the story I am indebted to Eta Linnemann, op. cit., pp. 58–64 and 143–146.

Four   Tomorrow Now

1. Philo, *Depraemiis et poenis*, 161–165.
2. E.g. *Book of Enoch*, 1–36. These chapters, known as *The Book of the Watchers*, form the earliest section of this composite collection and were probably written between 250 and 200 BC. *The Sibylline Oracles*, Book III, which originates from the second century BC. Also *Tobit* 14.5–7.
3. E.g. *Psalms of Solomon* 17 and 18. But, precisely because the image of the Messiah has featured prominently in Christian understanding of Jesus, we need the reminder of E. P. Sanders that a Davidic King 'is one of the least frequent themes in Jewish literature' (E. P. Sanders, *Jesus and Judaism*, SCM Press 1985, p. 117.
4. The 'millenial' idea of limited duration appears in II Baruch 40.3 and in IV Ezra 7.28–33. Both these apocryphal books are generally dated in the reign of Domitian (81–96 AD) or even later, but their ideas may have been current earlier.
5. E.g. *Assumption of Moses*, chs 7–10. This was the work of one of the Essenes at the end of the first century BC. Possibly also *Book of Enoch* 37–71 (known as *The Similitudes of Enoch*).
6. Lucas Grollenberg, *Jesus*, SCM Press 1978, p. 43.
7. The only occasion on which the three Synoptic Gospels all report Jesus as using the phrase 'enter the Kingdom' is the saying about the camel and the needle's eye (Matt. 19.23,24; Mark 10.23; Luke 18.25). In the saying about becoming as little children, Mark and Luke speak of receiving the Kingdom (Mark 10.15; Luke 18.17); it is Matthew who uses the term 'enter' (Matt. 18.3), and this may reflect his tendency to identify the Kingdom more closely with the life to come. On this score his other two uses of 'enter' (Matt. 5.20 and 7.21) may have been similarly altered.
8. Its local name, in Hebrew and Arabic, is Neve Shalom/Wahat al Salaam.

Five   Eating and Drinking

1. J. H. Charlsworth (ed.), *The Old Testament Pseudepigrapha*, Darton, Longman and Todd 1985, Vol. I, p. 44.
2. In the index to the two-volume collection edited by Charlsworth, noted above, there is only one other reference under Messianic banquet (Vol. I, p. 302), which comes from II Baruch 29.1ff. and speaks not of a banquet but of plentiful food. In any case II Baruch

is generally dated several centuries after Jesus.

3. Eta Linnemann, op. cit., pp. 96f.

4. Geza Vermes, *The Dead Sea Scrolls in English*, Penguin 1965, pp. 81, 121.

Six   The Narrow Road

1. Edwin Muir, 'The Road', from *Collected Poems*, Faber and Faber 1960, p. 223. Used by permission.

2. C. H. Dodd, *The Interpretation of the Fourth Gospel*, CUP 1953, pp. 241–249.

3. C. F. D. Moule, *The Origin of Christology*, CUP 1977, p. 12

4. Contrary to previous teaching that still enjoys wide circulation, New Testament scholars seem now to be in general agreement that the expectation of a Davidic Messiah is one of the least frequent themes in the Jewish literature of the period. The title was probably claimed by the leaders of some of the short-lived insurrections, and those who sympathized with the Zealots were quickly stirred by any rumour of a 'King' – which is essentially what the word meant. According to the Gospel of Mark, the victims of demon-possession sometimes gave Jesus the title, and Peter used it in his confession at Caesarea Philippi. But Jesus himself disparaged the popular claimants, silenced the possessed and, in Mark's account of Caesarea Philippi, forbad the disciples with a note of reproof to publicize the claim in those terms (the word *epitimao*, changed, always implies a rebuke). He never, in the Synoptic Gospels, spoke of himself as King, for the King was always God in his understanding, and he was the servant of that Kingdom by living already under the perfected sovereignty of God. But since the Servant in the prophesies in Isaiah was anointed for his special role, Jesus could accept the title of Messiah in that sense. He immediately gave it that sense at Caesarea Philippi, and Mark makes that moment the turning point of the Gospel. The triumphant entry, 'humble and seated on an ass', underlined that meaning. And it was after the resurrection, when they understood that meaning, that his followers began to call him openly, the Christ.

5. C. F. D. Moule, op.cit. pp. 13–22. Also T. W. Manson, *The Teaching of Jesus*, CUP 1935, p. 227.

INDEX